COLORADO MOUNTAIN COLLEGE

1 03 0002246967

D1626934

DISCARDED

GT2295 .A35 H35
Hair in African Art and
Culture

DISCARDED

DATE DUE

ILL May 2015		

Demco, Inc. 38-293

COLORADO MOUNTAIN COLLEGE
Quigley Library
3000 Cty. Road 114
Glenwood Springs, CO 81601

Hair

in African Art and Culture .

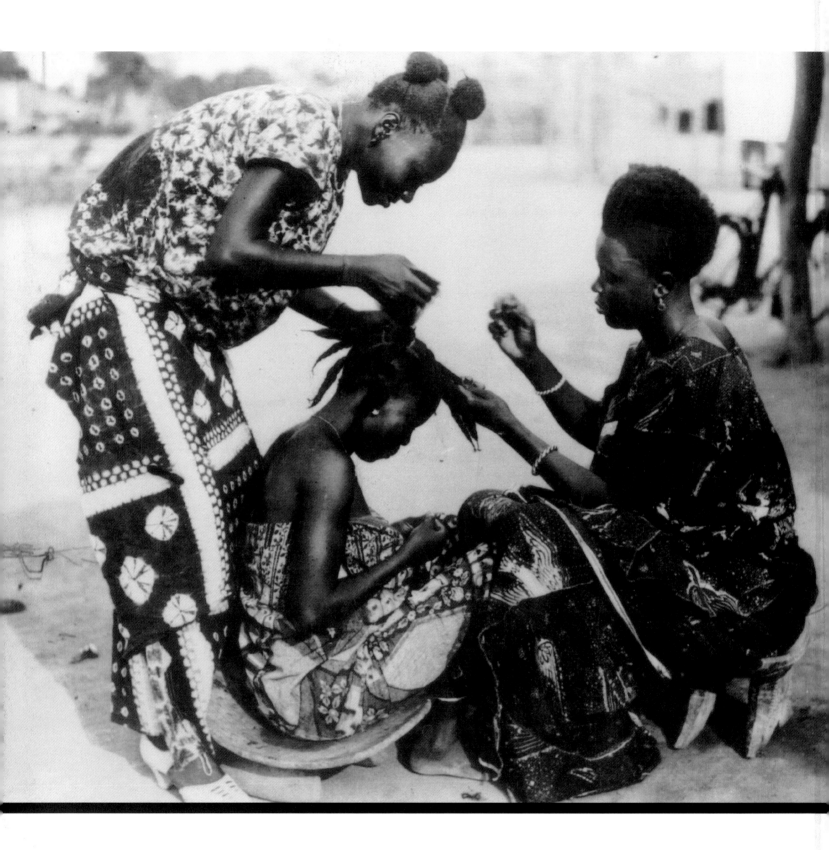

Hairdressing in West Africa.
Photograph courtesy Afrika Museum, Berg en Dal.

Hair

in African Art and Culture

Edited by ROY SIEBER and FRANK HERREMAN

with contributions by:

Niangi Batulukisi
Elze Bruyninx
Els De Palmenaer
Kennell Jackson
Manuel Jordán
Babatunde Lawal
Karel Nel
Mariama Ross
William Siegmann
Barbara Thompson
James H. Vaughan

THE MUSEUM FOR AFRICAN ART, New York
PRESTEL, Munich, London, New York

HAIR IN AFRICAN ART AND CULTURE is published in conjunction with an exhibition of the same title organized and presented by the Museum for African Art, New York from 9 February to 28 May 2000. The exhibition will travel to The Apex Museum, Atlanta;
Iris & R. Gerald Cantor Center for Visual Arts, Stanford University; Charles H. Wright Museum of African American History, Detroit; and California African-American Museum, Los Angeles. The national tour of *Hair in African Art and Culture* is sponsored by Colgate-Palmolive company.

The exhibition is supported by grants from the National Endowment for the Arts, a federal agency, and the Rockefeller Foundation.

Associate Curator: Laurie Farrell
Copy Editor: David Frankel
Translators: Gert Morreel, essays by Els Bruyninx, Else de Palmenaer, Frank Herreman from Dutch; Joachim Neugroschel essay by Niangi Batulukisi from French

Copyright 2000 © Museum for African Art.
All rights reserved. No part of this publication may be reproduced without written permission from the Museum for African Art, 593 Broadway, New York, NY 10012.

Copyright 2000 © Joachim Neugroschel.
All rights reserved. English translation of essay by Dr. Niangi Batulukisi,
"Hair in African Art and Culture."

Prestel books are available worldwide. Please contact your nearest bookseller or write to either of the following addresses for information concerning your local distributor:

Prestel Verlag
Mandlstrasse 26
80802 Munich, Germany
Phone (49 89) 381 7090, Fax (49 89) 381 70935

4 Bloomsbury Place
London WC1A 2QA
Phone (0171) 323 5004, Fax (0171) 636 8004

16 West 22nd Street
New York, NY 10010, USA
Phone (212) 627 8199, Fax (212) 627 9866

Library of Congress catalogue card no. 99-068113
Clothbound ISBN 3-7913-2291-5
Paperbound ISBN 0-945802-26-9

Cover design: Linda Florio Design.
Lay out by Annick Blommaert
Printed, and bound in Belgium by Snoeck-Ducaju & Zoon.

Front cover: Photograph (fig. 86): Fulani woman, French Guinea, early 20th century.
Cat. 129. Crest mask. Zombo, Angola and Democratic Republic of Congo.
Cat. 46. Crest mask. Cross River, Calabar area, Nigeria.
Cat. 158 (detail). Barber shop sign. Ghana.

Back cover: Fig. 8: Hairstyle of adult women. Kwaluudhi and Ngandjera of the Wambo Group, Namibia, 1940s. Fig. 117: Child in Burkina Faso, 1999. Field photo: Barbershop, Ghana. Ernie Wolfe, III, 1998.

Contents

Current donors

INDIVIDUAL

Mr. & Mrs. Charles B. Benenson
Jane & Gerald Katcher
Ms. Kathryn McAuliffe
Mr. Don H. Nelson
Lynne & Robert Rubin
Daniel Shapiro & Agnes Gund
Cecilia & Irwin Smiley
Mr. Jason H. Wright

Mr. & Mrs. Armand P. Arman
Bernice & Sidney Clyman
Mr. Edward Dandridge
Mr. & Mrs. Richard Faletti
Mr. Irwin Ginsburg
M.J. & Caral G. Lebworth
Drs. Marian & Daniel Malcolm
Mr. & Mrs. James J. Ross
Jerome & Ellen Stern
Mr. & Mrs. Victor Teicher

Mr. & Mrs. Lewis B. Cullman
Mr. Rodney M. Miller
Dr. & Mrs. Bernard M. Wagner
Harold & Maureen Zarember

Mr. S. Thomas Alexander, III
Dr. & Mrs. Samuel Berkowitz
Dr. & Mrs. Oliver Cobb
Mr. & Mrs. Carroll Cline
Kurt & Mary Delbanco
Dr. Barbara Eisold
Ms. Meredith Finch
Dr. Suzanne Frye
Mr. & Mrs. Jacques Germain
Denyse & Marc Ginzberg
Mr. Lawrence Gussman
Mr. & Mrs. Stephen Humanitzki
Helen & Martin Kimmel
Diane & Brian Leyden
Donald & Florence Morris
Ms. Denise Murrell
Mr. Michael Oliver
Ms. Veronica Pollard
Mr. & Mrs. Marvin Ross-Greifinger
Mrs. Harry Rubin
Ann & Paul Sperry
Mr. & Mrs. Saul Stanoff
Mr. De H. Guillaume Vranken
Mr. Richard White

Mr. & Mrs. Paul L. Abbott
Mr. & Mrs. Gerald D. Abrams
Mr. & Mrs. Arnold Alderman

Ms. Susan Allen
Robert R. Banks
Walter & Molly Bareiss
Ms. Saretta Barnet
Ms. Joan Barist
Dr. Jean Borgatti &
    Dr. Donald Morrison
Mr. Edward R. Bradley, Jr.
Ernest P. Bynum &
    Dennis M.Costin
Ms. Linda Cahill
Mr. Jeffrey Cohen &
    Ms. Nancy Seiser
Ms. Annette Cravens
Lisa & Gerald Dannenberg
Ossie Davis & Ruby Dee
Ms. Margaret H. Demant
Dr. D. David Dershaw
Drs. Jean & Noble Endicott
Toni G. Fay
Mr. & Mrs. Steve Felsher
Ms. Nancy D. Field
Ms. Vianna Finch
Ms. Diana R. Gordon
Dr. & Mrs. Gilbert Graham
Mr. Anthony Haruch
Ms. Joyce A. Kuykendall Haupt
Ms. Mary L. Heider
Ms. Barbara Hoffman
Mr. Stuart Jackson
Mr. & Mrs. Bernard Jaffe
Mr. Lloyd Sheldon Johnson
Teri Kearney
Mr. Lawrence Klepner
Mr. Luciano Lanfranchi
Mr. & Mrs. Guy Lanquetot
Mr. Jay T. Last
Mr. & Mrs. Samuel Lurie
Ms. Mary Ellen Meehan
Mrs. Kendall A. Mix
Dr. Werner Muensterberger
Mr. Peter Mullett &
    Ms. Heather Heinlein
Ms. Rhoda Pauley
Ms. Sandra Packer Pine
Kenneth & Bettina Plevan
Mr. & Mrs. Fred M. Richman
Ms. Beatrice Riese
Mr. & Mrs. David Ross
Mr. & Mrs. Arthur Sarnoff
Mr. Sydney L. Shaper
Ms. Mary Jo Shepard
Dr. & Mrs. Jerome Siegel
Cherie & Edwin Silver
Mr. & Mrs. Kenneth Snelson
Mr. Lucien Van de Velde
Ms. Mary Wagner
Dr. & Mrs. Leon Wallace
Mr. Willet Weeks

George & Joyce Wein
Ms. Margaret L. Wells
Michelle & Claude Winfield
Mr. John F. Zulack

**CORPORATE,
FOUNDATION & GOVERNMENT**

The Buhl Foundation, Inc.
City of New York Department of Cultural
Affairs
The Chase Manhattan Corporation
Colgate-Palmolive Company
The Culpeper Foundation
The Max and Victoria Dreyfus Foundation
Lannan Foundation
The LEF Foundation
Metropolitan Life Foundation
National Endowment for the Arts
The New York Community Trust
New York State Council on the Arts
RJR Nabisco Foundation
The Rockefeller Foundation
U.S. Department of Housing and Urban
Development
Zeneca Pharmaceuticals

ABC, Inc.
American Express
Bell Atlantic Foundation
Consolidated Edison Company of New York, Inc.
The Irene Diamond Fund
The Equitable Foundation
J.P. Morgan Charitable Trust
William H. Kearns Foundation
The M.J. & Caral G. Lebworth Foundation
May & Samuel Rudin Foundation
The Peninsula Foundation
Philip Morris Co.
Jill & Marshall Rose Foundation
Shelley & Donald Rubin Foundation, Inc.
Texaco, Inc.
Henry van Ameringen Foundation

Ambac Assurance Corporation
Dime Savings Bank
The Gordon & Llura Gund Foundation
Merrill Lynch & Co.
New York Council for the Humanities
Putumayo World Music
State Farm Mutual Automobile Insurance
Company
Tiffany & Co.
Toyota Motor Corporation

Current as of November 17, 1999

Board of trustees

Robert Rubin
Jason H. Wright
Co-Chairs

Jane Frank Katcher
Vice Chair

Kathryn McAuliffe
Secretary

Richard Faletti
Assistant Secretary

Lofton P. Holder, Jr.
Treasurer

Corice Canton Arman
Charles B. Benenson
Sherry Bronfman
Edward Dandridge
Irwin Ginsburg
Lawrence Gussman
Lawrence Klepner
Lee Lorenz
George Lumsby
William Lynch, Jr.
Rodney Miller
Dikembe Mutombo
Don H. Nelson
Veronica Pollard
James J. Ross
Irwin Smiley
Dennis D. Swanson
Victor Teicher
Phyllis Woolley

Staff

Executive
Elsie Crum McCabe
President

Anne Stark
Deputy Director

Ana Pelaez
Executive Assistant

Jerome Vogel
Senior Advisor

Curatorial

Frank Herreman
Director of Exhibitions

Laurie Farrell
Associate Curator

Barbara Woytowicz
Registrar

Carol Braide
Curatorial Assistant

Development

Amy M. Johnson
Membership Coordinator

Education

Radiah Harper
Deputy Director of Program & Education

Melissa Maldonado
Becky Morettini
Laurella Rinçon
Betsy Steve
Education Interns

Finance

Andrei Nadler
Controller

Marketing

Samara Rubinstein
Marketing Associate

Operations

Ivan J. Moffitt
Security Director

Lawrence Ekechi
Winston Rodney
Maxwell Bart
Lawrence Kendle
Juanita Perry
James Johnson
Errol Goring
Security

Fitz Caesar
Building Manager

Retail

Anthony Cooper
Museum Store Manager

Michela Belfon
Anita Burrows
Carolyn Evans
Zenzele Harvey
Ogoa Pierre C. Koffi
Sales Associates

Andre Norfleet
Stock Shipping

Volunteers

Joan Banbury
Coordinator of Volunteers

Cosima Amah
Olga Kovalchuk
Nathaniel Stepney
Svetlana Tarasova
Museum Store Volunteers

Narkide Andre
Mark Chenault
Kristine Cioffi
Nojamba Filomena Cornelio
Salimah El-Amin
Samuel Forbes
Lisa Hammel
Avis Hanson
Lois Henderson
Rebecca Herman
Bill Horn
Joanna Hunter
Hassan Adam Jojo
Zainab Sumu Koroma
Monique Littles
Christopher Logan
Natasha Mangoaela
Shirley Marc
Brenda McQueen
Dena Montague
Trevor Palmer
Xavier Rivera
Mary Cathryn Roth
Jennifer Scott
Mark Shoffner
Naoko Watanabe
Claude L. Winfield
Docents

Preface

It's your crowning glory, the top of your knot, the pinnacle of your person, your icing on the cake. It's your hair and you don't feel good unless your hair looks good. But what does it say about you? Your life? Your personal style? Your place in the community? In African society, it speaks volumes, reflecting differing cultures and identifying social and religious status and functions.

Consider the differing hairstyles found on adolescents before and after undergoing pivotal ceremonies of initiation; the distinctive hairdos that connote status and authority within a group; the ways in which hair, added to a sculptural figure, can activate a supernatural being incarnated through the object. Add to these elements the spectacle and beauty of elaborately adorned coiffures, many of which take not only hours but days to create—and no wonder hair is then also an item to protect!

This examination of hair in African art and culture is both an academic eye-opener and a delightful subtle turning of the mirror toward our own contemporary attitudes toward hair. One might come away from this exhibition with a new appreciation for the voice of hairstyles in our own society as well, and with a keener eye with which to observe the statements these styles make.

To enable this marvelous show, many people have devoted time, expertise and resources. To Exhibition Curator Roy Sieber of the University of Indiana, who worked side by side with the Museum's Director of Exhibitions Frank Herreman, we extend our deep appreciation for sharing his many years of accumulated knowledge, perception and insight. A heartfelt thank you also to the many lenders who have entrusted their precious pieces to this traveling exhibition so that audiences throughout the United States may experience the pleasure they give. Of course, none of this would be possible without the tireless efforts of the entire Museum staff, whose caring attention to producing outstanding exhibitions and educational programming makes all that we do possible. Thank you one and all for your hard work and commitment to excellence.

Special acknowledgment must be given for the generous sponsorship provided by the Colgate-Palmolive Companies which is making the national tour of this exhibition to Atlanta, Stanford (CA), Detroit, and Los Angeles both a possibility and a reality. The creativity and vision of Colgate in this partnership are a spectacular and inspiring example of how the public and private sectors can work together to bring art and ideas to new audiences everywhere.

Lastly, we thank the National Endowment for the Arts and the Rockefeller Foundation for providing funds in support of this exhibition. In addition, grants from the New York State Council for the Arts and the Department of Cultural Affairs enable program development that reach our immediate community.

Elsie CRUM McCABE
President
Anne H. Stark
Deputy Director

Acknowledgments

It is a great pleasure for us to acknowledge the people involved in the production of the exhibition *Hair in African Art and Culture*. During the last eighteen months we worked closely with several scholars who provided precious information. Therefore, our special thanks goes to the essayists in this catalogue: Niangi Batulukisi, Elze Bruyninx, Els De Palmenaer, Kennel Jackson, Manuel Jordán, Babatunde Lawal, Karel Nel, Mariama Ross, William Siegmann, Barbara Thompson, and James Vaughan.

We would also like to thank several museum curators including Mary Jo Arnoldi, National Museum of Natural History, Smithsonian Institution; Diane Pelrine, Indiana University Art Museum; John Nunley, The Saint Louis Art Museum; Rita Sá Marques, National Museum of Ethnology, Lisbon; Victoria Rovine, University of Iowa Museum of Art; and Jan Van Alphen and Els De Palmenaer, Etnografisch Museum, Antwerp. Our special thanks goes to Rosyln Walker, Director, and Janet Stanley, Chief Librarian, National Museum of African Art, Smithsonian Institution.

This exhibition would not have been possible without the willingness of the many collectors to lend their artworks. The lenders are: Corice and Armand Arman; Alan Brandt; Pamela and Oliver E. Cobb; Charles and Kent Davis; Drs. Jean and Noble Endicott; Etnografisch Museum, Antwerp; Felix Collection; Mona Gavigan/Afffrica; Marc and Denyse Ginzberg; The Graham Collection; Rita and John Grunwald; Toby and Barry Hecht; Henau Collection; William M. Itter; Indiana University Art Museum; Reynold C. Kerr; J.W. Mestach; Rolf and Christina Miehler; Charles D. Miller III; Mr. and Mrs. Donald Morris; Amyas Naegele; National Museum of African Art, Smithsonian Institution; Michael Oliver; Roy and Sophia Sieber; Joyce Marie Sims; Merton Simpson Collection; Thomas D. Slater; Cecelia and Irwin Smiley; Saul and Marsha Stanoff; Richard White; Ernie Wolfe Gallery; The Saint Louis Museum of Art; The University of Iowa Museum of Art; and others who wish to remain anonymous.

We wish to thank the Board of Trustees at the Museum for African Art, Elsie Crum McCabe, President; and Anne Stark, Deputy Director. Our gratitude goes to all staff members and volunteers. A special thanks goes to Laurie Farrell, Associate Curator, Barbara Woytowicz, Registrar, and Carol Braide, Curatorial Assistant and Publications Coordinator. We also thank Meredith Palumbo who assisted in the preparation of the catalogue.

The field photographs have been provided by Christaud M. Geary, Curator of Eliot Elisofon Photographic Archives at the National Museum of African Art, Smithsonian Institution; Mrs. Cornelia Eisenburger, Director, and Irene Hübner, Collections Manager, Afrika Museum, Berg en Dal, Holland; The Tervuren Museum, Belgium; and Evan Schneider who printed and kindly gave us permission to publish his father's photographs.

We would finally like to thank our wives Sophia Sieber and Saskia Verheijen who lovingly endured continuous conversations about hairdos, wigs, and beards since the idea for this exhibition crystallized more than two years ago.

Roy SIEBER
Guest Curator
Frank Herreman
Co-Curator and Director of Exhibitions

Hairdressing

Hairdressing in Africa is always the work of trusted friends or relatives.
In addition to the amiable social aspects of the event, the hair, in the hands
of an enemy, could become an ingredient in the production of a dangerous
charm or "medicine" that would injure the owner.

Usually women dress the hair of women and men dress the hair of men.
In 1721, however, Atkins offered one of the rare early descriptions of the
process of hairdressing reporting that the women of Sierra Leone
"work hard at Tillage, make Palm-Oil or spin Cotton, and when they are free
from such work, the idle Husbands put them upon braiding, and fettishing
out their woolly hair (in which Sort of Ornament they are prodigious proud
and curious), keeping them every Day, for many Hours together, at it"
(Astley II:319). [R.S.]

ABOVE
Fig. 1. Creating a hairdo for an annual dance,
Mambila, Cameroon.
Photo: Gil Schneider, 1948, courtesy of Evan Schneider.

LEFT
Fig. 2. Creating a coiffure,
West Africa.
Photo: Afrika Museum, Berg en Dal.

OPPOSITE
Fig. 3. Women, Cameroon.
Photo: Hector R. Acebes, 1953. Courtesy Hector R. Acebes.

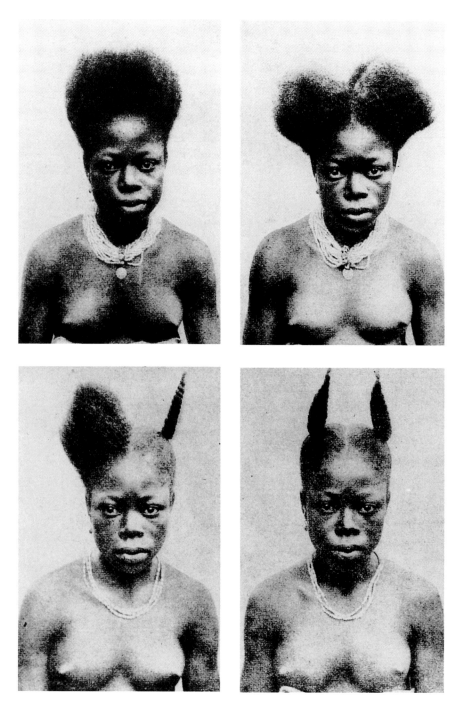

Fig. 4. Various stages of coiffure-making,
Fanti, Ghana, early 20th century.

Cat. 1
Figure
Fanti, Ghana
Wood, fabric, beads. H: 111.8 cm.
Private Collection, Los Angeles

Prologue

Roy SIEBER

The exhibition *"Hair in African Art and Culture"* and this volume serve to introduce a mode of African art too little and too infrequently recognized or appreciated. Field photographs and traditional sculptures sample the rich variety of hair arrangements that exist or have existed in African life and art.

Despite the many references to the abstract character of African sculpture there are two areas of the real world that almost without exception were depicted accurately, indeed often realistically: scarification and coiffures. Both can serve to identify ethnic origin, gender, phase of the life cycle, status, as well as personal taste. It must be emphasized that all hair styling, historical or modern African and African-American, has a major aesthetic component.

Essays, notes, and interludes address some of the concerns and aspects of African and African-American hair. Collectively they only hint at the richness, variety, and history of hairstyles. Some of the essays are personal, some present the nature of coiffures in the cycle of life: from birth to death, from celebration to mourning. Some focus on the moment in the life of a girl or boy during initiation, others scan the role of hair in establishing identity during the lifetime of a member of a particular ethnic group, and one reviews the comments and descriptions of early travelers.

Scholars, missionaries, colonials, and travelers with an interest in Africa have long been aware of the variety, often the richness, of both men's and women's hair arrangements. Most often they were best informed about the people with whom they were primarily concerned. The authors in this volume for the most part reflect that local knowledge, focusing on one group or several culturally or geographically related groups.

However, more generally shared attitudes or beliefs emerge from the essays. For example, hair may reflect an unusual or abnormal condition. M.O. McLeod notes among the Asante, "Priests' hair was allowed to grow into long matted locks in the style known as *mpesempese* (a term sometimes translated as 'I don't like it') (fig. 5). Uncut hair is usually associated with dangerous behavior: madmen let their locks grow, and the same hair style was worn by royal executioners" (1981:64).

OPPOSITE
Fig. 5. Healer, Côte d'Ivoire.
Photo: E. Laget, 1974.

Unshorn locks are visible in the photograph of the Dan warrior (fig. 6). As McLeod notes they may also be the sign of a mentally handicapped person, as with the naked adolescent male this author saw in northern Ghana in the mid 1960s. Although locally described as "mad" he was nevertheless tolerated, indeed protected, by the entire village. Both the nudity and the unkempt hair were symptomatic of the unsocialized status of the young man. In Ibadan, Nigeria, in 1971, an adult woman termed "mad" was observed dancing estatically, uncoiffed and nude along the main road to Ife. She appeared during the first showers of every rainy season.

Mourning is often expressed by deliberately abandoning normal, carefully coiffed hair. In Ghana, "No sooner has the breath left the body than a loud wailing cry bursts forth from the house, and the women rush into the streets with disordered clothes and disheveled hair, uttering the most acute and mournful cries" (Ellis 1887:237). A similar state is seen in the photograph of the Mangbetu widow shown in fig. 82, P.122.

Other general observations would include hair as a reflection of one's place in the cycle of life, one's status, or one's special condition as a leader. Hair can be protective when small patches are left on the fontanel of an infant (see fig. 10, P. 27) whose head is otherwise shaved. The soft area of unfused bones on the skull—the fontanel—was believed to be an entry point for dangerous spirits and would be protected by the patch of hair.

In several essays it becomes clear that high status was often reflected, indeed expressed, in the styles of complex coiffures. Yet William Siegmann in his essay notes that older Dan women of high status wear less elaborate styles than young women, and J. H. Vaughan reports that older Margi women and men shave their heads.

As noted by many of the authors, styles change; what was fashionable a week, a year, or perhaps as long as a generation ago gives way to new forms, which in turn will one day be replaced.

Many styles that are depicted in early photographs or sculptural forms have been abandoned. For example the Shilluk man's style illustrated in fig. 7 was "unfashionable" by the early 1930s (Seligman and Seligman 1932:38).

Unfortunately, except for a few such hints, much of that history is lost to us. We can but observe the present or read the records of the recent past. It is important to realize that today's observer can note and record what is observed in only a brief snippet of time. It is equally important to realize that that has always been so, for we note what is a moment in the flow of fashion.

Undoubtedly some changes were introduced from outside Africa via Islam or Europe, yet internal change in fashion is indicated by the differences that exist between closely related groups living at no great geographical distance from each other.

A primary tool for shaping and teasing the hair is of course the comb. As Max Schmidt notes, "The comb is found among every people of the world, and appears in

Fig. 6. Warrior with amulets in his hair, Dan, Liberia.
Photo: Himmelheber, 1950.

numerous forms" (1926:67). He goes on to state that "treating the hair with butter or vegetable oils is a widespread practice, and so is rubbing with earth or lime" (ibid.). Oils and agents such as camwood and ochers are used to dress the hair or shape the coiffure, as are devices such as extensions of human hair from spouses or relatives, or of vegetable fibers, or, more recently, of locally spun or imported mercerized cotton. Hair is often stitched over supports of bamboo, wood, or basketry. Further, razors and picks are used in creating complex hairdos. Perfumes such as lavender, sandalwood, and frankincense may be added, and ornaments of beads, gold, shells, buttons, seeds, and ivory may adorn hair arrangements or wigs.

Certain aspects of hairstyles—braids, tresses, chignons, or wigs—may be very old. Ancient Egyptian tomb reliefs show forms similar to those observed and photographed in the last century; many are identified as wigs. Indeed one touching example is a small wig on the mummy of a seven-year-old girl who died of typhoid, which had caused her hair to fall out (Brier 1998:45).

Boris de Rachewiltz, in *Black Eros*, makes numerous references to parallels among hairstyles in sub-Saharan Africa and Pharaonic Egypt (1964: e.g., 130–31). Unfortunately, little evidence exists to link the provocative examples observable in ancient Egypt and Nubia with many of the more recent coiffures recorded in the photographs and sculptures to be seen in this exhibition.

Fig. 7. Man with elaborate hairdo, Shilluk, Sudan.
Photo: Bernatzik, first half 20th century.

History

Roy SIEBER

As Kennell Jackson notes in his essay 'What is *Really* Happening Here?" (p. 175), the early traveler Pieter de Marees commented on African men's hair styles as early as 1602. Although rare, references in the writings of early travelers are nevertheless frequent enough to argue convincingly that hair arrangements were a serious concern by Africans for more than the past three centuries. It may be assumed with certainty that that concern was far older than the European notices.

A major compendium of early sources is *A New General Collection of Voyages and Travel*, assembled by Thomas Astley and published in four volumes in 1745–47. Although his intended scope was the whole world, a major portion of the first three volumes was devoted to Africa. He attempted to survey in a straightforward manner all major published voyages to which he had access.

A discussion of the extensive "borrowing" (often pirating) of information by early authors can be found in Hair, et al, (Eds) *Barbot on Guinea*, 1992. They offer quite a list of plagiarizers! However the editors note that "in respect to critical analysis, Astley's collection of voyages was outstanding and ahead of its time" (xcviii). Much of what follows derives from what has come to be known as 'Astley's Voyages.'

References to hair are found relating to the cycle of life. Shaving the head of an infant is common in most of sub-Saharan Africa, as has been noted in several of the essays and is reflected in the photographs. In Senegal, Francis Moore notes that at about a month and a half old "they Name the Child, by shaving its Head and rubbing it with Oil, inviting five or six Friends to be Witnesses" (1730 in Astley II:275).

The role of hair in coming-of-age ceremonies is exceedingly rare in early reports. However, Barbot (about 1700) describes the initiation activities of the "Sandi" society on what was then called the Grain or Pepper Coast (modern Sierra Leone and Liberia). He reports that the oldest woman of the society is sent by the King to "rule and govern the [initiation] School," which usually lasts four months. "Then she shaves their heads. . .", After which they are instructed in the dances of the country (Astley II:542; see Siegmann's essay).

Astley states that Cado Mosto's "Voyages [1455] are remarkable for being the oldest extant that we meet with . . . ." (I:574). Thus what is possibly the earliest European reference to men's and women's hair is in his description of the Jalofs of the south side of the Senegal River: "Both sexes go bare-footed and uncovered, but weave their Hair into beautiful Tresses, which they tie in various Knots, though it be short" (Astley I:582). Writing of the men of the neighboring Azanaghi: "They wear their Hair, which is black, frized over their Shoulders, like the *Germans*; and oil it every Day with the Fat of Fish, which makes them smell very strong; yet they repute it very modish" (Cada Mosto, 1455, in Astley I:579).

Possibly the earliest European reference to beards is that of Azambuja, who in 1494 established Elmina, the first Portuguese fort on the Gold Coast (modern Ghana). He describes the leader Karamansa, "King of Guinea," whose legs and arms were covered with plates of gold. "About his Neck he wore a Chain, with many small Bells and Tags to his beard" (Astley I:16–17).

Later reports from the area of the Senegal River offer rather fuller descriptions of coiffures and often refer to the use of ornaments. For example, Brüe in 1715 describes the coiffures of two sisters of a king:

> *Their Hair was dressed behind in the Shape of Bodkins ["long pins used by women to fasten up the hair (1580)" OED] which hung down the neck from Ear to Ear. They were adorned at the Ends with Bits of Coral and Gold, by way of Fringe. Their Hair over the Forehead was raised like a Tuft, or Pyramid, by means of Cotton underneath; and the Forepart separated and laid-down like that of the French Country Girls. The Extremities, which were curled, lay in Buckle, ["the state of hair when crisped and curled (1789)" OED] Part on the Forehead and Temples, and Part round the Ears, which were uncovered to shew their pendants: Those of the married Princess being large Pieces of Coral, and of the other, Rings of Gold. Their Eyebrows were very black, which they kept up, by rubbing them often with a Piece of black Lead. They affected much to shew their Hands and Nails, which were very large, and red at the Ends; Things by them reckoned great Beauties (Astley II:129).*

Brüe also describes the hair ornaments of a female Senegalese musician (*Guiriot*) whose hair was loaded with small silver amulet boxes as well as trinkets of gold, silver, coral, and amber.

Men among the Peul (Fulani, in Astley: Fulis) of the Senegal River area "are proud of their Hair, which they affect to cut into different Shapes." Some "let their Hair grow long, plaiting it like a Horse's Mane on which they string Coral or Pipe-Beads. Many (especially up the river) wear on their Crowns a good number of small Horse-Bells" (Moore, 1731, in Astley II:214). Peul women "like yellow Amber, Drops of Gold or Glass of that Colour: They make Chaplets and Knots of them, dressed upon Cotton, which they stick in their Hair, and looks quite pert and genteel" (Brüe, 1697, in Astley II:63).

"Jobson informs us that upon the Head [the Senegalese] wear [amulets] in the Form of a Cross, from the Forehead down behind to their Neck and from Ear to Ear;

likewise about their Neck and cross both Shoulders round their Middles, their Arms and above and below the Elbow; So that they carry a whole Load of religious Blessings" (Jobson, 1621, in Astley II:301).

There are numerous references to the hairdressing and ornaments among the Wolof, Fuli, and Mandingo along the Senegal River. For example: "They dress their Hair, which is short, very prettily, with *Grisgris* [amulets], Silver, Leather, Coral, Copper, Etc. . . . Those descended of Slaves are not allowed to wear their Hair." Or: "Their Hair is also decked with Coral, and other little Baubles. Their Head-dress makes a sort of Coif, half a Foot high, the higher, the handsomer" (Jannequin, 1643, in Astley II:271).

Finally, there is the comment by Brüe (1697) that women of high status "never scratch their Head when it itches, but with a golden Bodkin" (Astley II:65). A complex hairdressing compounded of tresses and plaits, decorated with beads and other ornaments, when completed, is both dense and long-lasting. There is no other way to scratch the scalp except with a pin or bodkin.

Few descriptions of hair from along the West Coast of Africa are to be found in the writings of the early travelers. There are references to the men of the Bissagos Islands dressing their hair with palm oil, which colors it "quite red" (Brüe, 1701, in Astley II:104, 106).

In describing the dress of the peoples of Sierra Leone, Finch, 1607, states: "Their Beards are short, crisp, and black. As to the Hair of their Heads, some cut it in cross Lines, leaving square Tufts standing; others wear it jagged in Tufts, or in other Forms; but the Women shave all close" (Astley II:305).

Also on the Grain Coast on the River St. Vincent, both the men and women "for the most part . . . go bare headed, their Hair being clipped, and shaved in various Manners" (Towrson, 1555, in Astley I:152). Snoek (1702) notes that men and women in the Grain Coast plaited and braided their hair. "Both take great Delight in twisting the Wool of their Heads into Ringlets with Gold or Stones, and bestow a great deal of Time and Genius in it" (Astley II:523).

Atkins notes that the inhabitants of Cape Apollonia on the Ivory Coast have their hair "twisted in numberless little Rings and Tufts, with Bits of Shell, Straw or Gold twisted in them" (1721, in Astley II:558).

In the late seventeenth century Barbot (1679) noted that the peoples of the Ivory Coast:

> . . . . *wear long locks of hair, plaited and twisted, which they daub with palm oil and red earth. This hair is the hair of their wives, which they cut off and tie it this way, end to end, and fix it on their heads; some let it hang down, others turn it up! There are some who by this means make their heads look so large that from a distance one would say they were [wearing] large bonnets!* (Barbot, I, Letter 31: 301).

About a decade later Phillips (1693) observed a similar process of extending the hair. However, instead of human hair, "They plait some Flax into their Hair, making a small Sinnet from each Lock which hangs down to their Shoulders: Some tie them up in a Roll behind . . . and others, on the top of Head" (Astley II:395).

Sinnet is a sailor's term: "A kind of flat braided cordage formed by pleating together several strands of rope-yarn, coarse hemp, grass, etc" (1611, OED).

Are these references the earliest descriptions extensions and dreadlocks?

Echoing the descriptions of the hair ornament of the Senegal River area:

> MARCHAIS observes, that there are few Negresses [on the Ivory Coast], but have their Hair adorned with little Toys of pure Gold, in which the Workmen of the Country shew their Skill. These they call *Manillas*, a general Term with them, equivalent to the Word *Jewels*, in Use among *Europeans*. These *Manillas* are of various Forms, generally very slight and thin; but the Wives of the rich Negroes have such a Quantity of them on their Heads, as amounts to a considerable Value: Nor does a young, handsome Negress make an ill Figure, so adorned. The Husbands, however, who in this Country have more Authority than in *France*, make no Scruple to strip their Wives of these Ornaments, and sell them for such Goods as they want (Marchais 1715, in Astley II:561).

The early references to Karamansa and his decorated beard have been noted. Various ornaments were used to decorate the hair of the inhabitant of both the Ivory Coast (Côte d'Ivoire) and the Gold Coast (Ghana). Summarizing the reports of Marchais (early 1700s) and Bosman (late 1600s) on the peoples of the Gold Coast, Astley states:

> The Dress of the richer Sort is various, especially with respect to their Heads, in which they take the greatest Pride; but this is the Business of their Wives. Some wear their Hair very long and curled and plaited together, or tied up to the Crown: Others adjust it in small Curls, smeered with Palm-Oil, and a Sort of Dye, which they order in the Form of a Rose, or Crown; decking it with Gold Toys, and a Kind of Coral, called on the Coast *Conta de Terra*, which they sometimes value three Times beyond the finest Gold. They use also for Ornament a Sort of blue Coral, called by the *Europeans, Aqrie*, by the Blacks *Akkerri*, which brought from *Benin*; and, when of any Bigness, is prized equal with Gold, and sold for Weight. Some shave-off all their Hair, leaving only one Part, about an Inch broad, and in the Shape of a Cross, or a Halft Moon, or Circle. They also wear in their Hair, one or more small narrow Combs, of two, three, or at most four, sharp Teeth, being like a Fork without a Haft, or Handle: This they thrust through their Crowns or Roses of Hair when they are bitten by Vermin; scratching themselves thus, without discomposing their Head-Dress, which would require some Time to adjust again.
> Some let their Hair . . . grow, and others shave it often, according to their different Customs. Usually the young People shave often, and every Morning wash their Heads, and nib them over with Palm-Oil, ... (Astley II:631).

From the Slave Coast (now the Republic of Benin and Nigeria) Marchais (1725) reports that the women of Whidah, once a major trading center, "dress their Hair genteely, and with Art, adorning their Locks with Gold Spangles, and bits of Coral or

Beads" (Astley III:17). Describing the hair of the men and women of the Kingdom of Benin, Nyendael (about 1699) states:

> THE Men content themselves with letting their Hair grow in its natural Form, except buckling it in two or three Places, in order to hang a great Coral at it. But the Womens Hair is very artificially curled-up in great and small Buckles; and divided on the Crown, like a Cock's Comb inverted, by which Means the small Curls lie in exact Order. Some divide their Hair into twenty or more Curls, as it happens to be thick or thin; others oil it with Palm-oil: By this Means its black Colour turns, in Time, to a Sort of Green or Yellow, which they are very fond of, though, in the Author's Opinion, it looked hideously (Astley III:96).

Writing of the peoples along the Rio Gabon, Artus (really de Marees?, 1602) reports:

> They all go bare-headed, having their Hair strangely cut or tied-up. Some have small Caps made of Twigs, or the Bark of the Cocoa; others have Bundles or Feathers fastened with Iron Wire or Plates (Astley III:124).

There are only minimal references to the hair arrangements of the men and women of the Kingdom of Congo. Pigafetta in 1591, for instance, only notes that some have "black Curly hair, and others with red" (p. 13). Barbot a century later reports that the Prince of Soni "was sitting in a great Chair, his head newly shaved . . . ." (Astley III:204).

In contrast, Merolla (1682) is far more detailed when he reports that the people of the Loango Kingdom

> wear their Hair according to their Quality: The Queen had hers shaved close on the Crown, and little Tufts left all round on the Sides. Some have it shorn in a circle like that of a Monk, and others have theirs plaited down in Points towards their Foreheads and their Necks; insomuch, that if there were the least straggling Hairs, they would be cut away, and the rest shaved close to the Head.
> (Astley III:218).

The peoples of southern Africa, collectively called the "Hottentots," were the subject of an account by Kolben in 1713. He offers the following reference to hair:

> In hot Seasons the Hottentot Men go bare-headed, their usual Plaister of Soot and Fat excepted. With this, they load their Hair every Day, and it gathers so much Dust and Filth, which they leave to clot without ever cleansing it, that it looks like a Crust, or Cap, of black Mortar. This, they say keeps their Heads cool. In Winter they wear Caps, or rather Bonnets of wild Cat, or Lamb Skins. . . . women wear Caps in all Seasons, Day and Night (Astley III:351).

He adds that they "are very fond of Ornaments for the Head. They first took a Fancy to Brass-Buttons and little thin Plates of the same Metal, which continue in

fashion at the *Cape* to this Time. Bits of Looking-Glass are in high esteem with them
. . . . " (Kolben in Astley III:352). Kolben also tells of a most unusual hair ornament: a
man who has killed a lion, leopard, elephant, or rhinoceros is considered a hero. He
is honored by the other men. At the end of a three-day celebration he "rejoices with
his friends and Neighbors; wearing ever after the Bladder of the Beast he has killed,
fastened to Hair, as a Mark of Honour" (Astley III:356).

Attitudes toward hair during periods of grief and mourning are also reported
infrequently in the early literature. Marchais (1725) notes that the women (wives and
relatives?) of a deceased village chief on the Grain Coast were loud in their lamenta-
tions, all the while tearing their hair and scratching themselves (Astley II:545).

There are a number of instances where widows and other relatives shaved their
heads as an expression of mourning, among them the peoples of the Gold Coast,
Benin Kingdom, and South Africa (Astley I:661, III:97, III:361).

The body of the deceased is usually washed and groomed. Loyer (1701)
describes for the Ivory Coast what may have been a typical practice. Women after an
initial period of lamentation "paint, comb, and curls [the deceased's] Hair, and adorn
him with his Pagne [wrapper] and Jewels" (Astley II:439).

Fig. 8. Hairstyle of adult women.
Kwaluudhi and Ngandjera of the
Wambo group, Namibia.
Photo: Annaliese Scherz, 1940s.

Hair in African Art and Cultures

NIANGI Batulukisi
Translated from the French by Joachim Neugroschel

Both in everyday African life and in African sculpture, hair has always been one of the body parts receiving the most care and attention. The earliest European travelers and explorers were struck by the diversity of African hairstyles. The presence of coiffures on artworks inspires admiration as well as questions about their nature, use, and function. The present essay aims at offering a few answers by focusing on sub-Saharan Africa, where a certain unity of culture provides the basis for the aesthetics of coiffures. The hairstyles discussed are part of a long tradition and still preserve their old symbolism and their quality as attributes of the gods. Hairstyles in ancient Egypt often closely resemble more recent examples south of the Sahara; others are to be found in the terracotta figures from the Nok and related cultures about 2000 years ago.

A biological component of the human body, hair has become a cultural element of social communication. Perceived as the expression of a cultural identity, a social status, or a profession, the traditional coiffure has multiple purposes. Some serve to identify the wearers or to bring them respect for the functions they perform; others might define a temporary state or might serve as an ornament in or a necessary part of the dance.

Without denying the skills of contemporary individuals, we have to emphasize that in the past there were no professional hairdressers like those who practice in the African cities of today. Among those who still follow the old traditions, a person's choice of a coiffeur or coiffeuse is dictated by a friendship or family relationship, since giving someone the responsibility for your hair is an act of trust. (The fear that some of your clippings might fall into the hands of a person who wished you evil, and who could use them to do you harm, justifies the greatest possible care in selecting the person who will do your hair.) In this tradition, the craft of hairdressing, which is practiced by either sex, requires training with an experienced stylist. The young apprentices work only on children and on youngsters their own age; adults or children are worked on by other adults. The long styling session, lasting anywhere from several hours to several days, permits the stylist and the client to exchange private

OPPOSITE
Cat. 2
Figure: *ibeji*
Yoruba, Nigeria
Wood, metal, beads, fiber. H: 32.5 cm.
Private Collection, Belgium

25

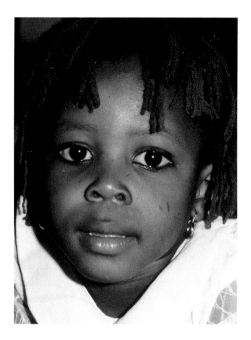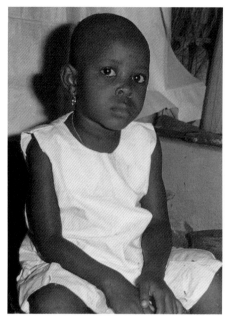

Fig. 9. Before and after views of a young girl with *ihiagha* (dread locks). According to Benin religion, the deity Olokun (god of the waters) sends followers to earth to be his devotees. One sign of this calling is the appearance of a special kind of curl that marks the child as an Olokun devotee (those of the other deities have a different kind of curl). Being born with *ihiagha* requires a life as a priestess, observing many taboos. Nowadays, parents may prefer that their children get an education. The young girl in these photographs is depicted before and after she has undergone the ritual to remove *ihiagha*, a ritual which is both expensive and highly dangerous because the deity may take offense. A village Olokun priestess with the same kind of hair is shown in the third photograph. Benin, Nigeria, 1976. *Photo: Courtesy of Paula Girshick.*

information, or to talk about the life of the village. A mother might instruct her marriageable daughter about her future role as a wife, and so on.

The hairdresser's tools are rudimentary: a wooden or ivory comb for untangling the hair; a pin—made perhaps from a porcupine quill, perhaps from wood, bone, metal, or ivory—for tracing the partings, or for decorating the final hairdo; rags or vegetable fibers; grease or other hair ointments; a traditional knife and razor for shaving.

Hair care in traditional Africa is above all aesthetic in its goals. There is in black Africa an undeniable link between coiffure and beauty; a well-tended head has always been a criterion of beauty, a source of admiration, a reason for pride. A beautiful coiffure ennobles a woman or a man. Men are not indifferent to the sight of a well-coiffed girl or vice versa. If your hair is poorly looked after, conversely, you may be criticized and insulted, or worse: you may be called a lunatic, an outlaw, a witch doctor, an evil spirit. The opposition between nature and culture is thoroughly in play here: the transformation of hair shows the human desire to modify nature, to create. Hairstyling, then, is truly an artistic discipline.

Equally important is the tie between hair and magic. The association of hair with death and disease, on the one hand, or with sexuality, fertility, and vitality, on the other, is to be found among many African peoples. Numerous peoples shave their heads when grieving the death of a close relative/husband, wife, child, brother, sister—and the new hair that grows in is left unkempt until the mourning period is over. In magic, hair is understood as a surrogate for or extension of the person from whom it comes (Leach 1958:162). Thus if a person dies far from home, and his corpse cannot be shipped back, some hair is cut from the top of the head and placed in a box (a substitute for the coffin), perhaps along with clippings from the toe- or fingernails. This box is then sent to be buried in the deceased's native soil.

Similarly, at the end of a healing rite, the healer may shave the patient's head and put some of the hair into a charm that will guarantee recovery and protection.[1] The *mpungu* charm employed by the Yaka, the Yanzi, and the Teke as a receptacle for forces that promote health, or that bring power over others, is an anthropomorphic wooden figure incorporating hair from someone who is ill, or from the intended victim of witchcraft (see Tayeye 1979:285–87). Hair also plays a part in respecting the dead: among the Bwende of the Democratic Republic of Congo and the Beembe of the People's Republic of Congo, a deceased person is immortalized in an anthropomorphic statuette containing his nails and a bit of his hair. These statuettes, representing the dead and guaranteeing their postmortem presence among their near and dear, are both homes for and memories of the dead.

Throughout sub-Saharan Africa, the cutting of a child's hair for the first time demands a ritual, which differs from place to place. In western Africa, the baby's mother carefully keeps the cut hair in a basket (see Tayeye 1979:20, Baduel and Meillassoux 1975:11–12). Such precautions are justified by the fear that the hair, likened to the soul, may fall into the wrong hands.

Certain traditions call for a person to keep his hair long, even neglect it. Among the Yoruba, for example, twins (*ibeji*) and infants born with lots of hair (*dada*) must leave their hair long until it is cut in a special ritual (fig. 9). The children's hair symbolizes the wealth and prosperity that they are thought to bring their parents; flouting this prohibition would bring misfortune on the child (Houlberg 1971:375–77). Yoruba artists make the virtues of twins tangible in statuettes with high-crested hairdos or with high chignons (cat. 2).

A man's head is often clean-shaven. A child may wear a tuft of hair on a partially shaven cranium (fig. 10). At puberty, the time of the rites of initiation and circumcision, his head is shaven completely, after which he can wear his hair like an adult.

A coiffure is perfected by various decorations: cowries, beads, mother-of-pearl buttons, medals, pieces of silver, amber balls, metal rings, and pins of wood, bone, or ivory. A man may adorn his display coiffure with feathers. For purposes to do with magic, a man or woman may also attach amulets to certain hairdos. The more elaborate coiffures include braids, crests, curls, cascades, chignons, and vertical cornrows.

In the West African Sahel, the Fulbe and the Peul (Fulani) cultivate impressive hairstyles (fig.11). Peul girls wear very tight longitudinal braids going from forehead to nape and falling down the shoulders and the back, while transversal braids emerge from the sides of the head. An adolescent girl has tight braids separated by fairly symmetrical partings, and a coiled tuft on either side of her head. Adult women of lower rank have two raised transversal braids and also small parallel braids on either side and separated by a part down the middle.[2] High-ranking women may have their own hairstyle, an intricate combination of braids interpolated with more or less thick coils distributed in front, in back, and on the sides of the head.

In western tropical Africa, the most impressive female coiffures that have survived in sculpture consist of braids enriched with curls and false elements made of vegetable fibers—the preludes to the crest hairdo still worn today. In such hairdos the crest is raised, either crosswise or lengthwise. The crosswise crest can be found in the Gulf of Guinea (Baduel and Meillassoux 1975:197), among the Mende (Liberia), the Dyala (Ivory Coast), the Ashanti, the Yoruba, the Mossi, the Bamana, the Lobi, and others. The crest goes from ear to ear, and the remaining hair is shaved or finely plaited in small braids, their number and location being based on the

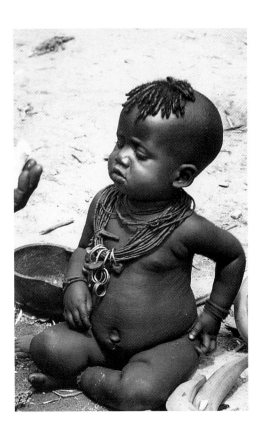

Fig. 10. Child with fontanel protection. Mambila, Cameroon.
Photo: Gil Schneider, 1950, courtesy of Evan Schneider.

Cat. 3
Staff
Senufo, Côte d'Ivoire
Wood, cowrie shells, gold, leather, fiber.
H: 117.6 cm.
Private Collection

Fig. 11. Woman with complex coiffure and
hair ornaments, Fulani, West Africa.
Photo: Afrika Museum, Berg en Dal.

Fig. 12. Woman with coiffure in the form
of a crest with ornaments and comb,
Igbo, Nigeria.
Photo: Afrika Museum, Berg en Dal.

woman's status. The longitudinal crest is also found among the Mende (see Siegmann, page 71). It is widespread among the Peul, the Fulbe in Chad, and the Bassani of Guinea. It also extends its influence as far as the Tikar of Cameroon (Bernolles 1966:12), and appears on wooden Dan figures, on Guro masks, on Baule masks and sculptures, on Yoruba depictions of women and horsemen, and on certain Dogon masks and figures (see cat. 38, p. 44). A crest is worn in a variety of circumstances: at a celebration of young people getting married, for instance, an Igbo woman in Nigeria wears a special hairdo of braids crested in the center, with flat braids on the sides, as a symbol of her new status (fig. 12). A Yoruba bride wears an enormous crest on her wedding day, while an Igbo woman styles her upswept hair to signal the birth of a first child.

The elite warrior of the Senufo wore a longitudinal crest, with a pompom at each of the two ends. This crest was topped off by two features: one was a pair of lateral braids, each emerging from the hair above either temple and dropping to the shoulders; the second was an additional braid forming a tail to the crest. This coiffure is even more striking in a female ancestor figure representing a mother and child (cat. 3).[3]

Women of East Africa usually wear their hair cut short, or have their heads shaved. Children wear a crest going from the forehead to the nape of the neck; the rest of the head is shaved. The nomadic shepherds in the great lake's region of Uganda, Rwanda, Burundi, Kenya, Tanzania, and the eastern part of the Democratic Republic of Congo are distinguished by a tuft on the front of the head (Paulme and Brosse 1956:57). The Maasai wear a multitude of small braids arranged in a border at the front of the head, over the temples, and in back (fig. 13). Among the Nilo-Hamitic population we find a large chignon, among the Bantu peoples a medium-sized chignon, and in Uganda and the Sudan a spherical hairdo. The Maasai coiffure of a raised tail in the back of the head was adopted by the Bantu. Certain Zaramo (cat. 5) and Doe sculptures (Tanzania) show crests that imitate the hairstyles of children.

Fig. 13. Maasai man, Tanzania.
Photo: Hector R. Acebes, 1953.
Courtesy of Hector R. Acebes.

Some are adorned with human hair. The naturalism of Makonde artists (cat. 4) leads them to depict and use human hair on masks and figures.

In central Africa, both men and women sport a wide variety of coiffures: twisted hair, braids, crests, chignons, cascades. Twisted tresses thickened with oil and red powder, in which the hair falls to the shoulders, the temples, or the forehead, are described early (fig. 14). A hairstyle of tiny curls treated with red clay can be found on Angolan masks and statuary (Chokwe, Lwena, Holo), where it is rendered as tiny diamond points, or as rows of several small pyramids in well-accentuated cascades covering the entire head (cat. 6). Various kinds of braids appear in the same region, comparable to those in West Africa. They have evolved toward more highly accentuated forms like the crest. We could cite countless examples of transversal crests in central African sculptures, but let us single out the heads on Kota reliquaries (Gabon), which sport the largest examples (fig. 15).

Northern Sotho women, in South Africa, may wear a type of crest hairdo in which the head is shaved on both sides and the median hair is pleated into very fine, tight braids in the form of a more or less flat crest going from forehead to nape. A hairdo with a longitudinal crest, known as *mukot* (or *mukoto*) appears frequently in Kwango-Kwilu in the Democratic Republic of Congo. It is also shared among many other sub-Saharan peoples, and is used to be worn by both sexes (figs. 16, 17). In this coiffure, several large crests going toward the back of the head are horizontally separated from one another by partings. This hairdo is also frequently depicted in Central African statuary (cats.7, 9)

Among the Tabwa, a coiffure made up of a long braid hanging down the back

Cat. 4
Head
Makonde, Tanzania
Wood, human hair. H: 16 cm.
Drs. Jean and Noble Endicott

Cat. 5
Hairpins
Zaramo or Kwere, Tanzania
Wood. H: 21.5 and 22.5 cm.
Private Collection

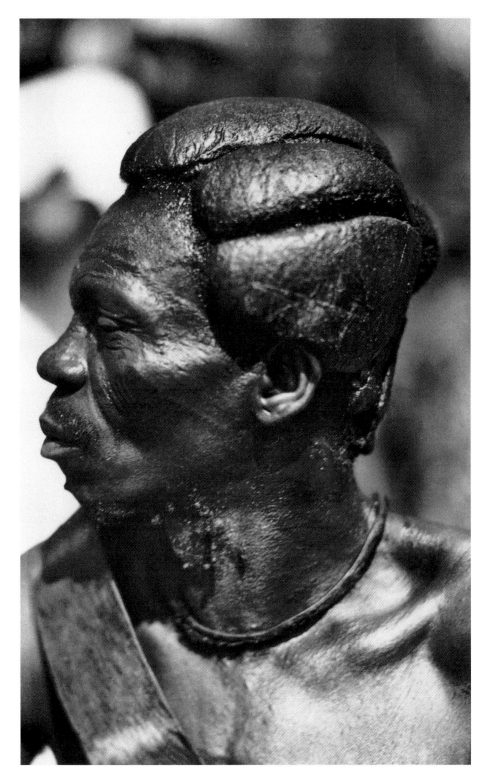

Fig. 14. Banza man,
Democratic Republic of Congo.
Photo: Zagourski, 1926–1937.

Fig. 15. Reliquary guardian figure.
Kota, Gabon. Wood, brass, copper. H. 67.3
cm. Buffalo Museum of Science.
Photo: Jerry L. Thompson.

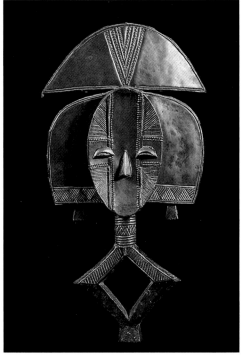

OPPOSITE
Cat. 6
Helmet mask
Holo, Democratic Republic of Congo
Wood, red khula, kaolin, charcoal
pigments. H: 39 cm.
Felix Collection

Cat. 7
Helmet mask
Mbala, Democratic Republic of Congo
Wood, metal. H: 29 cm.
Felix Collection

Fig. 16. Man with hair arrangement
typical for the area, Mbala or Pende,
Democratic Republic of Congo,
first half 20th century.

Cat. 8
Hat
Pende or Mbala,
Democratic Republic of Congo
Fabric, leather, metal. H: 26.7 cm.
Roy and Sophia Sieber

Fig. 17. Pende man,
Democratic Republic of Congo.
Photo: Zagourski, 1926-1937.

Cat. 9
Helmet mask
Yaka or Suku, Democratic Republic
of Congo
Wood. H: 29.2 cm.
The Saint Louis Museum of Art,
Gift of Marian D. May

Cat. 10
Hat
Yaka or Suku,
Democratic Republic of Congo
Fiber. L: 26.5 cm.
Corice and Armand P. Arman

33

Cat. 11
Figure
Tabwa, Democratic Republic of Congo
Wood. H: 26 cm.
Private Collection

Cat. 12
Fertility Figure/Doll
Tabwa, Democratic Republic of Congo
Wood. H: 17.5 cm.
Drs. Jean and Noble Endicott

 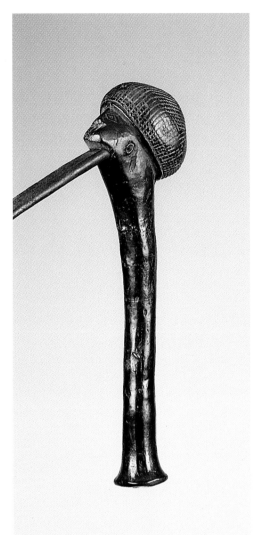 

Cat. 13
Adze
Luba Kasai, Democratic Republic
of Congo
Wood, iron. H: 36 cm.
Felix Collection

Cat. 14
Adze
Lele, Democratic Republic of Congo
Wood, iron. H: 34 cm.
Felix Collection

Cat. 15
Axe
Kaniok, Democratic Republic of Congo
Wood, iron, varnish. H: 38 cm.
Felix Collection

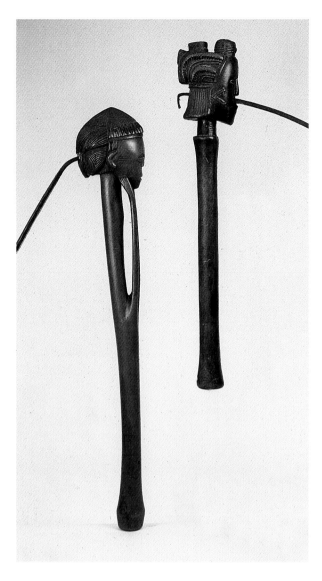

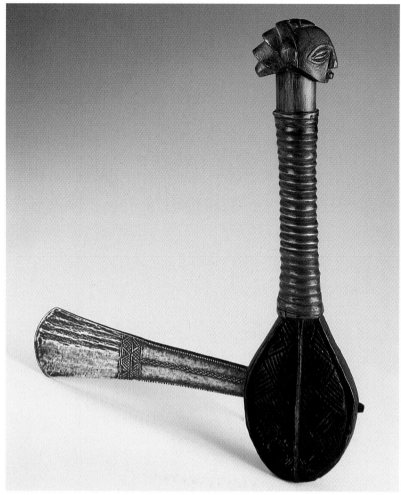

Cat. 16
Adze
Luba, Democratic Republic of Congo
Wood, iron. H: 48 cm.
Felix Collection

Cat. 17
Adze
Luba, Democratic Republic of Congo
Wood, iron. H: 40.6 cm.
Felix Collection

Cat. 18
Axe
Luba, Democratic Republic of Congo
Wood, iron, copper, brass. H: 35 cm.
Felix Collection

Cat. 19
Axe
Luba, Democratic Republic of Congo
Wood, brass tacks. H. 43.5 cm.
Felix Collection

(Roberts 1986:16) was formerly linked to a Buyanga society of hunters; this style is of major importance in Tabwa iconography (see de Grunne and Roberts 1985) (cats. 11, 12).

The complex hairstyles of the Luba (cats. 13-19) and related groups designate the high social status of their wearers. Certain hairstyles of Holo dignitaries vanished long ago, surviving only in a few sculptures. This is the case for a coiffure of two large pleats forming a crest and dropping on either side to the shoulders, seen in photographs of Chief Ndembo (Redinha 1975:fig. 9) and of Yaka and Suku chiefs (photographed by C. Lamote in 1950 and reproduced in Bourgeois 1982: 31, fig. 3). This coiffure also appears in Holo, Yaka, and Suku mask.

In most instances, these styles identify the wearer as belonging to the nobility; most of the statues or masks on which they appear depict chiefs, wives of chiefs, female chiefs, and queen mothers (cat. 20).

In traditional art objects, coiffures testified to an aesthetic activity integrated in ritual practices, and to the inextricable bonds between art and culture on the one hand, and between art and belie on the other. The sculptures portrayed with elaborate coiffures represent deities or top-ranking political or religious personalities.

The majority of the modes discussed here still resist the changes in present-day Africa, continuing to assert themselves in ever-growing varieties. But European contacts with Africa, and the introduction of Christianity and Islam, have brought new types while modifying certain ancestral practices. Other styles, such as the Afro and the curly, seen among modern Africans and African-Americans, have produced a symbiosis between tradition and modernism.

Hair stylists today express a certain freedom in interpreting signs, motifs, and cultural symbols. This trend appears more and more among contemporary artists who are moving away from the social conventions in which these hairstyles were created. Their preoccupations are purely aesthetic and artistic, yet they allow the artists to perpetuate the symbolic traditions of hair by reproducing ancient hairstyles.

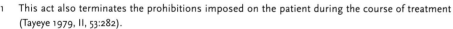

1   This act also terminates the prohibitions imposed on the patient during the course of treatment (Tayeye 1979, II, 53:282).

2   This style may be compared to the ancient Nubian coiffure of undulating parallel curls lined up on both sides of a median parting, as shown on a fourth-millennium (?) predynastic statue from Saharan Libya. See Capart 1956: fig. 8, p. 10.

3   See, for example, the Senufo statuette in the Stanley collection, published in Christopher 1985:24–25, fig 11.

Cat. 20
Figure
Luba, Democratic Republic of Congo
Wood, horn. H: 38 cm.
Felix Collection

Status or Identity: Spiritual or Secular

Many figures, masks, and prestige objects display complex coiffures.

They are often symbolic of the status of the ancestor portrayed, of the

significance of the spiritual force embodied by the masquerader, or of the

secular importance of a ruler. [R.S.]

OPPOSITE
Cat. 21
Cup
Kuba, Democratic Republic of Congo
Wood. H: 27.2 cm.
Indiana University Art Museum

Cat. 22
Figure
Luba, Democratic Republic of Congo
Wood. H: 43 cm.
Private Collection

Cat. 23
Figure
Guro, Côte d'Ivoire
Wood. H: 27 cm.
Private Collection, Belgium

Cat. 25
Figure: biteki
Yaka, Democratic Republic of Congo
Wood. H: 49 cm.
*The University of Iowa Museum of Art,
The Stanley Collection (CMS 425)*

Cat. 24
Figure
Madagascar
Wood. H: 104 cm.
Private Collection, Belgium

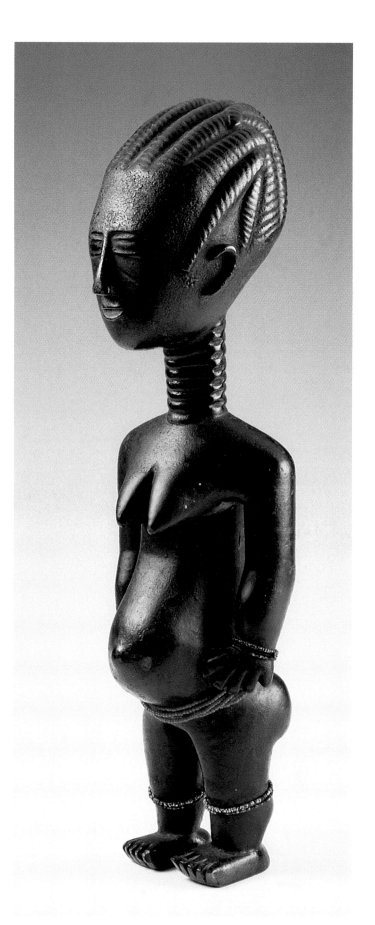

Cat. 26
Figure
Alangwa, Côte d'Ivoire
Wood, beads. H: 27 cm.
Richard White

Cat. 27
Figure
Ashanti, Ghana
Wood, beads. H: 37.5 cm.
Henau Collection, Antwerp

Cat. 29
Ancestor Figure
Bembe, Congo (Brazzaville)
Wood. H: 13.6 cm.
Private Collection

Cat. 28
Figure
Oron Ibibio, Nigeria
Wood. H: 64 cm.
Collection of Toby and Barry Hecht

Cat. 30
Pole Sculpture
Bongo, Sudan
Wood. H: 162 cm.
Private Collection

41

Cat. 32
Figure
Baule, Côte d'Ivoire
Wood, beads. H: 29.3 cm.
Private Collection

Cat. 33
Heddle pulley
Baule, Côte d'Ivoire
Wood. H: 20.5 cm.
Henau Collection, Antwerp

Cat. 31
Reliquary figure: *byeri*
Fang-Ntumu, Gabon
Wood. H: 39.4 cm.
Corice and Armand P. Arman

TOP
Cat. 34
Face mask
Igbo, Nigeria
Wood. H: 38.1 cm.
Private Collection

Cat. 35
Crest mask
Ejagham, Nigeria
Wood, skin, hair, basketry. H: 26 cm.
Henau Collection, Antwerp

TOP
Cat. 36
Helmet mask
Igala, Nigeria
Wood. H: 33 cm.
Collection of Toby and Barry Hecht

Cat. 37
Crest mask
Cross River, Calabar area, Nigeria
Wood, skin. H: 44.5 cm.
Collection of Toby and Barry Hecht

Cat. 38
Mask
Dogon, Mali
Fiber, cowrie shells, plastic beads, metal.
H: 58 cm.
*National Museum of African Art, Gift of D.
William H. Stewart*

Cat. 39
Heddle pulley
Baule, Côte d'Ivoire
Wood. H: 16.5 cm.
Henau Collection, Antwerp

Cat. 40
Adze
Luba, Democratic Republic of Congo
Wood, iron. H: 43 cm.
Felix Collection

Cat. 41
Adze
Unknown provenance
Wood, iron, black. H: 48 cm.
Felix Collection

OPPOSITE
Cat. 42
Crest Mask
Ejagham, Nigeria
Wood. H: 31 cm.
Private Collection

Hair: sculptural modes of representation

Frank HERREMAN

The field photographs included in the catalogue and exhibition offer convincing proof that the rich diversity of hairstyles is an important part of the daily personal care and aesthetics of men, women, and children in sub-Saharan Africa. As earlier described, coiffures are not restricted to the purely aesthetic but serve as a marker to distinguish between youth and adult, girl and boy, man and woman. Hairstyles also enable us to identify the social status and profession of their wearers.

In contrast to scarifications, coiffures and body paint are temporary. Body paint can be erased or may fade with time. Hair can be manipulated. It can be kept short or worn long. It can be braided or modeled with one or several crests, lengthwise or crosswise. Finally, it can be dyed or rubbed with different pigments or oiled. It is not surprising that hair works very well as a signifier.

The different possibilities are also represented in statues and masks. The manner of representation can for the most part be described as idealized. The proportions of many African statues are not realistic. Usually the head is extremely large in relation to the rest of the body. Most of the time this can be explained by the concept

Cat. 44
Fertility figure/doll
Kuba, Democratic Republic of Congo
Wood. H: 26.5 cm.
J.W. Mestach

OPPOSITE
Cat. 43
Face mask
Pende, Democratic Republic of Congo
Wood, knotted raffia, tukula, kaolin,
charcoal pigments. H: 22 cm.
Felix Collection

Fig. 18. A Pende man,
Democratic Republic of Congo.
*Photo: The Baptist Missionary Society,
early 20th century.*

Fig. 19. Boy playing "cat's cradle." Lele,
Democratic Republic of Congo.
Photo: Hans Himmelheber, 1938-39.

that the identity of the supernatural being or ancestor is largely determined by the shape, finish, and embellishment of the head. This includes scarification, facial paint, and the shape of the hair (cat. 45).

It is not difficult to point out extremes in hairstyle, ranging from minimal to elaborate and from rudimentary to extremely detailed, in the incredibly diverse formal language of African sculpture. Two examples illustrate this range. The hair line of the Kuba doll (cat. 44) is very minimal and is also a recurrent design element in ornamental cups, cosmetics boxes, and royal statues. The same coiffure can be seen in the photograph (fig. 19) of a boy from the Lele group, whose culture is closely related to that of the Kuba. At the moment the picture was taken, the higher hair line was still distinguishable; underneath it, however, new hair has begun to grow, which has to be trimmed regularly.

The crest mask from the Cross River region (cat. 46) contrasts sharply with the Kuba doll. The hair depicted on the mask is indisputably the center of attention. Several corkscrew braids radiate from the skull in different directions. Worn on the head of a moving masked figure, this coiffure helps to create a distinctly dramatic appearance. Most probably the mask was partly inspired by the kind of coiffure worn in a photograph of a woman from the Cross River region (fig. 20) This shows how a sculptor may use a particular hairstyle as a point of departure for the creation of one more fantastic.

Both these cases indicate that the African sculptor represents hairstyles concep-

ABOVE
Cat. 45
Figure
Igbo or Ejagham, Nigeria
Wood. H: 24 cm.
Collection of Toby and Barry Hecht

Fig. 20. A Cross River woman, Nigeria.
Photo: D. Mansfeld, early 20th century.

OPPOSITE
Cat. 46
Crest Mask
Cross River, Calabar area, Nigeria
Wood, skin. H: 56 cm.
Collection of Toby and Barry Hecht

Cat. 47
Amulet
Senufo, Côte d'Ivoire
Bronze. H: 17 cm.
Private Collection

Cat. 48
Figure
Ashanti, Ghana
Copper alloy. H: 10.2 cm.
Charles and Kent Davis

Cat. 49
Figure
Bamana (?), Mali
Iron. H: 14 cm.
Private Collection

Cat. 50
Figure
Bamana, Mali
Iron. H: 14 cm.
Charles and Kent Davis

ABOVE, FRONT AND BACK
Cat. 51
Crest mask
Anyang, Nigeria
Wood, skin. H: 33 cm.
Collection of Toby and Barry Hecht

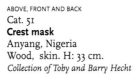

Cat. 52
Divination Tool
Luba, Democratic Republic of Congo
Wood. H: 30.5 cm.
Private Collection

OPPOSITE
Cat. 53
Face mask
Nguni River, Gabon
Wood, metal. H: 31 cm.
Private Collection, U.S.A.

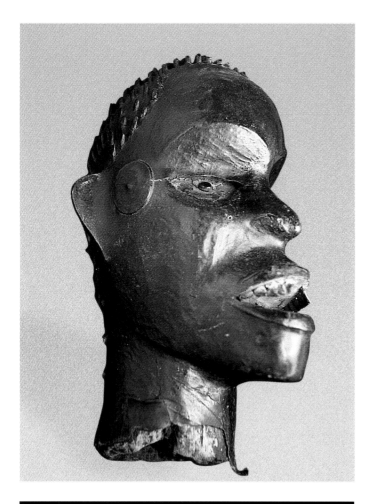

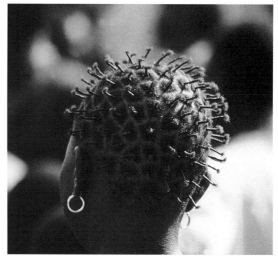

ABOVE
Fig. 21. Hairstyle. Njemetop, Nselle clan,
Cross River State, Nigeria.
Photo: Amanda Carlson, 1996-7.

Cat. 54
Crest mask
Ejagham, Nigeria
Wood, skin. H: 27 cm.
Rolf and Christina Miehler

Cat. 55
Figure
Songye, Democratic Republic of Congo
Animal hair, cowrie shells, metal.
H: 32 cm.
*Indiana University Art Museum,
Raymond and Laura Wielgus Collection*

OPPOSITE
Cat. 56
Crest mask
Idoma, Nigeria
Wood, fiber. H: 28 cm.
Collection of Toby and Barry Hecht

Cat. 57
Face mask
Igbo, Nigeria
Fiber, fabric. H: 38 cm.
Collection of Toby and Barry Hecht

Cat. 58
Face mask
Pende, Democratic Republic of Congo
Wood, fiber. H: 25 cm.
Felix Collection

Cat. 59
Mask
Kuba-Bushoong, Democratic Republic
of Congo
Rattan, cloth, fibers, beads, cowrie shells.
H: 24 cm.
Felix Collection

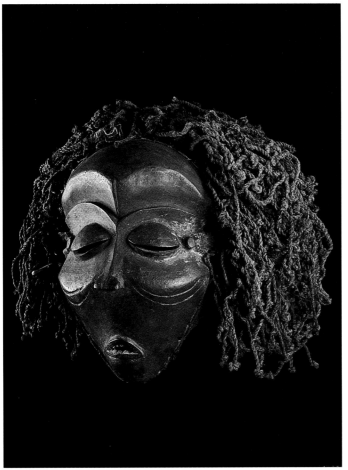

Cat. 60
Combs
Igbo, Nigeria
Ivory. H: 4 to 6 cm.
Amyas Naegele

Cat. 61
Crest mask
Keaka, Nigeria
Wood, skin, human hair, fiber. H: 29 cm.
Collection of Toby and Barry Hecht

tually rather than mimetically. This is entirely in line with one of the principal characteristics of African sculpture, which is that it never copies exactly from nature. Sculptors are more often inspired by what they know than by what they see. The artist does not hesitate to accentuate what is considered important in his culture.

The characteristics of a particular design are also determined by the materials used to make masks and statues. Wood, clay, or different metals such as copper alloys or iron each have their own characteristics, which influence the final shape. It is usually assumed that most of the sculptures are made of wood. A statue or mask is most often carved out of a block of wood. In order to hide the head of the wearer, raffia or cloth is attached to the mask. The sculptor uses an adze to carve the wood. Next, the finer work is done with a gouge or a small knife and subsequently the statue is polished. Color may be applied in different ways. To make the sculpture dark brown or black, the surface is scorched. The statue or mask can also be blackened by dousing it in mud and rubbing it afterward with plant juice or palm oil, which gives it a deep gloss. The sculptor chisels or carves a pattern, which may vary in depth, in a previously modeled volume (cat. 53).

Aside from sculpting and carving, hair can be made by other means as well. A coiffure can be suggested by coloring the head (cat. 51). Tufts of hair can be represented by putting wooden pegs in the head (fig. 21, cat. 54). In some cases, for instance among the Songye, iron arrowheads are inserted point downward into the head (cat. 55). A wig, usually made of raffia or knotted fibers, may be attached to the crown or temples of a mask. The shapes of these wigs are often inspired by actual coiffures, which serve as a basis for more fantastic hairstyles (cats. 56-59). Finally, there are also examples of the use of human hair attached to heads of masks or statues (cat. 61).

Representations of hair ornaments or amulets are also regularly included in sculpted coiffures. The lengthwise crest in Igbo *mmo* masks is often flanked on both sides by depictions of smaller, upright ornamental combs (cat. 60, 62). Coiffures and jewelry are almost inseparable in the sculpture of the Luba and the groups within their sphere of cultural influence, such as the Hemba (cat. 63). Their coiffures contain representations of metal plates, hairpins, and tiaras separating forehead and hair. Among the Luba, it is not uncommon to attach real beads to sculpted hair or to decorate it with a copper hairpin (cats. 64, 65). Sometimes, cowries are attached to the real hair of Cross River masks (cat. 66).

OPPOSITE
Cat. 62
Face mask
Igbo, Nigeria
Wood. H: 48.3 cm.
Collection of Toby and Barry Hecht

Cat. 63
Head of figure [front and back]
Hemba, Democratic Republic of Congo
Wood. H: 71 cm. [full figure]
Private Collection

Cat. 64
Axe
Kalundwe,
Democratic Republic of Congo
Wood, iron, aluminum, glass, beads,
varnish. H: 41 cm.
Felix Collection

Cat. 65
Knife
Luba, Democratic Republic of Congo
Wood, metal, fibers, beads. H: 19 cm.
Felix Collection

OPPOSITE
Cat. 66
Crest mask
Ejagham, Nigeria
Wood, skin, hair, cowrie shells. H: 26 cm.
Rolf and Christina Miehler

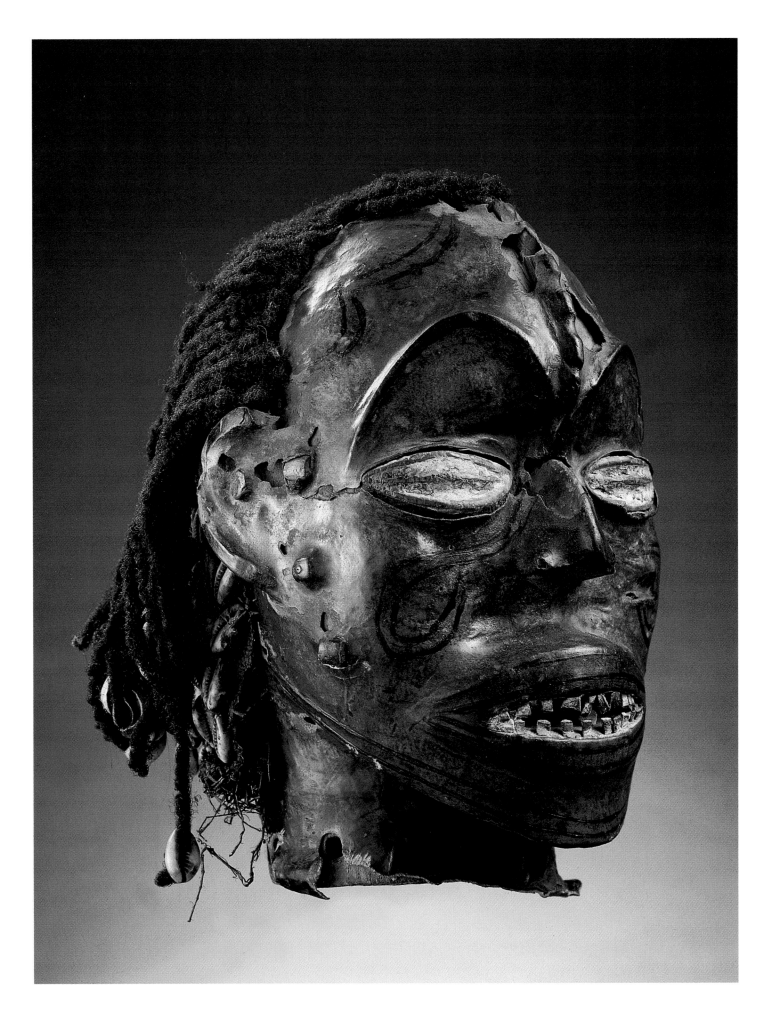

Wigs, Hats, Beards

Dressed human hair on the head is neither the only medium nor the only source of African hair representations. Wigs occur often, as do hats that echo the form of coiffures. Beards are common: they usually enhance the status of an adult male and reflect, when gray, the importance of an elder. References to the gray beards of West African elders and rulers appear from the sixteenth to the early eighteenth centuries. Perhaps the most elaborate reference to a beard is found in Loyer's 1701 description of the dress of the king of Issini (in the modern Côte d'Ivoire):

> His gray Beard was twisted into twenty small Locks, which were threaded with sixty Bits of Aygris Stone, bored, round and long. This is a kind of Precious Stone found amongst them, which has neither Lustre nor Beauty, and looks like our glass Beads; but these People esteem it so much that they give in Exchange its weight in Gold. By this Reckoning the King's Beard was worth a thousand Crowns (Astley II:422–23).

Bosman in the late 1600s offers an interesting note about the popularity of wigs:

> They are very fond of Hats and Perukes, which they wear, but after a Manner remarkably dismal. Formerly a great Trade was driven here by the Dutch Sailors in old Perukes, for which they got Wax, Honey, Parrots, Monkeys; in short, all Sorts of Refreshments whatever they pleased, in Exchange: But for these four Years so many Wig-Merchants have been here, that the Sailor swears the Trade is ruined (Astley III:124).

In Ghana in the mid-1960s, wigs were in great demand among women of high fashion. [R.S.]

Fig. 23. Woman with traditional hair style (*thihukeka*) made of sisal fiber. Mbukushu of the Kavango group, Namibia. *Photo: Anneliese Scherz, 1940s.*

Fig. 24. The wives of the Oba (the *iloi*) of Benin as well as high-ranking palace women and Olokun priestesses wear a special wig on ceremonial occasions. The wig is created by the women in the weavers' guild, Owina n'Ido, and is made of ram's hair and adorned with coral beads. It is called "chicken's beak." This photograph is of an Olokun priestess dressed as a queen for naming ceremony of the Peace Corps. Benin, Nigeria, 1976. *Photo: Courtesy of Paula Girshick.*

OPPOSITE
Fig. 22. Omahatela headdress, Mbalantu of the Wambo group, Namibia. *Photo: Anneliese Scherz, 1940s.*

Cat. 67
Wig
Mumbukush, Namibia
Leather, fiber, beads. H: 55.9 cm.
Michael Oliver

Cat. 68
Wig
Lega, Democratic Republic of Congo
Fiber, beads, coins, ivory, shells.
H: 30 cm.
Reynold C. Kerr

Cat. 69
Wig
Maasai, Kenya
Fiber, beads. L: 75.5 cm.
Merton Simpson Collection

OPPOSITE
Fig. 27. Hairstyles consisting of sinew
(eefipa), Mbalantu of Wambo group,
Namibia.
Photo: M. Schettler, 1940s.

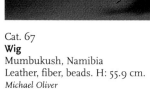

RIGHT
Fig. 25. Two women, southwestern Angola, 1958.
Photo: Centro de Informação e Turismo de Angola, Gabinete Fotográfico.

BELOW
Fig. 26. Two girls, southwestern Angola.
Photo: Courtesy of Affrica Archives, ex. collection, Janice Meyer Gordon.

Cat. 70
***Gle* head**
Wè, Côte d'Ivoire
Fiber, mushroom, boar tusk. H: 12.5 cm.
Charles D. Miller III

Cat. 71
Tunic
Grasslands, Cameroon
Fabric, human hair. H: 96.6 cm.
William M. Itter

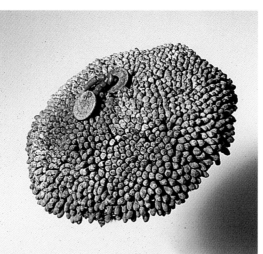

Cat. 72
Hat
Kirdi, Nigeria/Cameroon
Fiber, resin, earth, metal. H: 21.5 cm.
Amyas Naegele

Cat. 73
Hat
Zulu, South Africa
Fiber, beads, fabric. Diam: 40 cm.
Private Collection

Cat. 74
Hat
Zulu, South Africa
Hair. H: 45.7 cm.
Marc and Denyse Ginzberg Collection

OPPOSITE
Cat. 75
Medicine container
Grasslands, Cameroon
Calabash, basketry, human hair. H: 34 cm.
Michael Oliver

ABOVE LEFT
Cat. 76
Face mask
Wè, Côte d'Ivoire
Wood, metal, human hair. H: 43.2 cm.
Kate and Ken Anderson

ABOVE RIGHT
Cat. 77
Portrait mask
Wobe-Bete, Côte d'Ivoire
Wood, hair, fibers. H: 19.5 cm.
Corice and Armand P. Arman

LOWER LEFT
Cat. 78
Face mask
Dan, Côte d'Ivoire
Fiber. L: 46 cm.
Charles D. Miller III

LOWER MIDDLE
Fig. 28. Man with beard,
Balante, Guinea.
Photo: Bernatzik, first half 20th century.

LOWER RIGHT
Fig. 29. Tikar chief,
Ngambe, Central Cameroon.
Photo: Bernatzik, first half 20th century.

Cat. 79
Mask
Grassland, Cameroon
Wood, hair. H: 45.7 cm.
Roy and Sophia Sieber

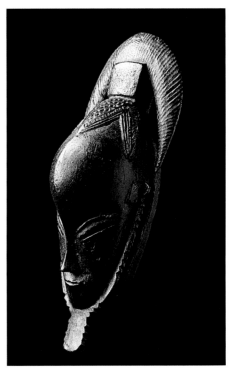

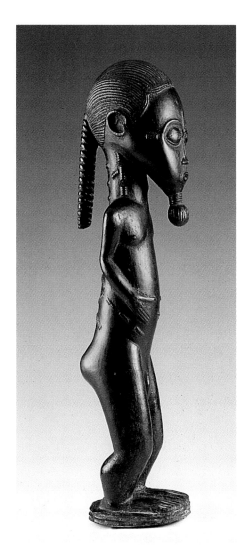

Cat. 84
Figure: *blolo bian*
Baule, Côte d'Ivoire
Wood. H: 43 cm.
Etnografisch Museum, Antwerp

Cat. 85
Ancestor figure
Bembe, Congo (Brazzaville)
Wood, fibers. H: 17.7 cm.
Private Collection

Cat. 86
Face mask
Baule, Côte d'Ivoire
Wood. H: 32 cm.
Henau Collection, Antwerp

OPPOSITE
Cat. 80
Face masks, portraits
Baule, Côte d'Ivoire
Male (left). Wood, fiber. H: 31 cm.
Female (right). Wood. H: 27 cm.
Private Collection, Belgium

Cat. 81
Mask
Kran, Liberia
Wood, fiber. H: 40.6 cm.
Charles and Kent Davis

Cat. 82
Face mask
Dan, Côte d'Ivoire
Wood, fiber, fabric. H: 38 cm.
Private Collection

Cat. 83
Face mask
Guro, Côte d'Ivoire
Wood. H: 43.2 cm.
Saul and Marsha Stanoff

Cat. 87
Comb
Baule, Côte d'Ivoire
Wood. H: 15.2 cm.
Charles and Kent Davis

Cat. 88
Comb
Somali, Somalia
Ivory. H: 5.7 cm.
Marc and Denyse Ginzberg Collection

RIGHT AND OPPOSITE
Cat. 89
Stool
Hemba, Democratic Republic of Congo
Wood. H: 37.3 cm.
Cecilia and Irwin Smiley

Women's Hair and Sowei Masks in *Southern Sierra Leone* and *Western Liberia*

William SIEGMANN

Few works of African sculpture are more focused on the depiction of hairstyles than are the *sowei* masks of the Sande women's initiation society, found among the Mende, Bullom-Sherbro, Temne, Vai, Gola, and Bassa in southern Sierra Leone and western Liberia. Worn by senior Sande officials, the sowei mask is at once the personification of the 'medicine' or power of the society, an incarnation of its tutelary spirit, and a representation of its collective leadership. The mask is also a representation of the ideals of feminine beauty, and as such its most distinctive feature is its elaborate treatment of the hair.

Somewhat ironically, women throughout this region are seldom seen in public without a head tie covering their hair. While the use of head ties may ultimately be due to Islamic influence, the covering of the hair is a social convention rather than a religious principle. Hair plaiting is done in the open and a woman's hair may be seen by anyone; yet a woman is not deemed properly attired without a head covering, much in the same way that properly attired European and American women once wore hats and gloves.

Beneath the head tie, however, is bound to be a carefully and beautifully coiffed head. In this region, few parts of the body are as central to the concept of feminine beauty as is hair. Sylvia Boone points out that for the Mende, hair has both physical and metaphysical properties associated with feminine beauty, and that a woman's hair should be "clean, smooth, shiny, well groomed, and plaited into a flattering style. Only a black color is acceptable. . . . brownish hair is thought to be dusty and dirty" (1986:96). A woman washes her hair every week and may treat it with an herbal mixture and oil it with palm oil. Somewhat surprisingly in a culture where age is highly respected and honored, both men and women may also dye their hair; gray hair is seldom seen.

On the metaphysical level, Boone notes that Mende women may liken hair to vegetation: both can grow and increase. A beautiful head of hair is one that is thick, lush, and abundant, like the rice in a well-tended field. A woman's coiffure encodes a

OPPOSITE
Cat. 90
Helmet mask: *sowei*
Mende, Liberia
Wood, raffia. H: 30.5 cm.
William M. Itter

71

Fig. 30. Some of the numerous styles in which the upper Mende women dressed their hair.
Photo: Alldridge, late 19th century.

prayer for abundant life and is thought of as demonstrating "the life force, the multi-plying power of profusion, prosperity, a 'green thumb' for raising bountiful farms and many healthy children" (ibid.: 186). A woman's thick long tresses symbolize fertility and strength. They are plaited together and bound at the ends into orderly configurations. In a sense, the plaiting of a woman's hair is a statement about her commitment to social order. Since a woman cannot plait her own hair, but must turn to a relative or friend to do it for her, the very act of plaiting one's hair is indicative of a social bond among women.

Disheveled hair, conversely, is symbolic of being in a state of disharmony with society. The insane signal their alienation from cultural norms and social integration by leaving their hair unattended. Only in bereavement does a sane woman indicate her estrangement and distress by removing her head tie and loosening her hair.

Thomas Alldridge pointed out at the beginning of the century that the most elaborate hairstyles were reserved for ceremonial occasions and were seen primarily on high-status women, such as the wives of chiefs, who had the leisure to have their hair elaborately dressed(1901:197). Today, generally speaking, younger women tend to wear more elaborate styles than older women. In part this may be because older women have less patience for the long hours needed to complete the tighter, more elaborate styles, and may also be less willing to put up with the discomfort felt from the tightly pulled hair of the more elaborate braids.

Though the terms 'braiding,' 'twisting,' 'plaiting,' and 'reverse braiding' are often used interchangeably, they actually describe different means of styling the hair. Hairstyles change over time, and those fashionable in one season may be out of fashion the next. Many basic hairstyles, however, persist from one generation to the next. The range of styles found in any given village today is undoubtedly broader than that found earlier in the century, but a photo taken at the end of the last century by Alldridge (1901:113) shows that fashion and individuality have always been features of hairdressing in the region (fig. 30).

The social bond symbolized in the plaiting of hair is nowhere more clearly seen than in a girl's initiation into the Sande society. The first phases of preparation for the 'bush school' in which the initiation will take place are all conducted by initiated women. They consist chiefly of ceremonies in which the Sande women take possession of the sacred grove where the rites will take place, and where the rice that will be used to feed the new initiates is publicly beaten. Initiated members conduct these ceremonies communally a few days before the initiation camp begins. The girls about to be initiated do not participate.

When the girls enter the bush school, it is night, and the town is 'closed' to men, who are not allowed outside as the girls leave. Earlier in the afternoon, however, the entire community is present for the public 'combing of the hair' of the prospective initiates, who gather with their friends and relatives in the center of the town. Each girl is brought here by an elder woman who may be a close relative or family friend, and who is in effect the girl's 'sponsor' for her initiation. This woman then sits on a mat and proceeds to comb the initiate's hair and plait it into an elaborate hairstyle (fig. 31). The styles are individualized and are said to have no symbolic significance in themselves. The activity, however, is symbolic of the initiate's first steps in participating collectively in the Sande society and in the bonds that women share.

Ironically enough, the first detailed account published on the Sande, by Olfert Dapper in 1668, states that the first thing that happens to a girl when she enters the initiation camp is that her head is shaved (1668:417). If this was once the case, it seems unlikely that such shaving is still practiced today, since the girls usually return from the bush school, after as little as four to six weeks, exhibiting a full head of hair. In any case, at the completion of the initiation camp the girls come back to their communities with elaborately plaited hair (fig. 32).

Once again these elaborate coiffures have a dual significance. On one level they are clearly meant to enhance a young woman's appearance and make her more attractive to perspective suitors. On another level they also signify the transformation that these girls have undergone by virtue of their initiation.

Throughout the region, people believe that the spirit world exists 'under the water.' It is from this realm that the *sowo-wui*, or sowei, the masked spirit of the Sande, emerges. When the girls are in the initiation camps they are also thought of as 'under the water,' and when they come back to the town their bodies are oiled, so that they shine as though they had newly emerged from water. The realm under the water is also one of perfection, and the hairstyles the girls exhibit as they return reflect this perfection in their elaboration and delicacy.

While there is some individual variation in the new initiates' hairstyles, the tendency is for all of the girls returning from a given camp to have similar styles. In some Gola, Vai, Mende, and Bassa areas, these are sometimes similar to the styles illustrated by Alldridge. In Loma and Bandi areas, on the other hand, the style is more likely to include long tresses that hang down in front to 'frame the face,' a style normally seen on older women.

The elaborate range of hairstyles found in both ceremonial and daily life is reflected in the variety of coiffures found on sowei masks. These coiffures are the masks' most sculpturally elaborated features and most distinctive elements of indi-

Fig. 31. Ma Kpanna dressing hair of Simo Bolay before entrance into Sande bush. Bandi, Bolahun, Liberia. *Photo: William Siegmann, 1981.*

Fig. 32. Sande Society initiates. Bandi, Bolahun, Liberia. *Photo: Patricia O'Connell, 1974.*

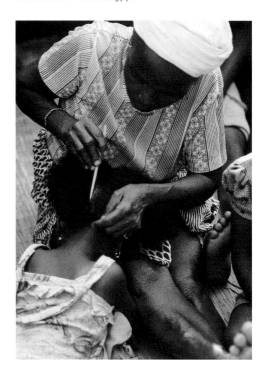

OPPOSITE
Cat. 91
Helmet mask: *sowei*
Mende, Liberia
Wood. H: 36.2 cm.
Woods Davy Collection

viduality. For the most part the coiffures are depicted with great precision. Finely incised lines indicate patterns of hair parting and braiding. The attention to hairstyling on the masks, and the wide range of hairstyles represented, suggests the intriguing possibility that it might be possible to trace a history of hairstyle fashion through the representation of coiffures on sowei masks.

In this respect Ruth Phillips has provided a wealth of information in her detailed study of Mende Sande masks in use in Jaiima-Bongor chiefdom, Sierra Leone, in 1972. She found that the oldest masks show hair arranged in a graduated series of high ridges running from front to back of the head. The number of ridges varies, but the most common numbers are one, three, five, and seven: "The number of ridges is always odd because of the interest in symmetry; there must be a central ridge originating at the apex of the triangle which describes the forehead and an equal number of ridges on either side. In most examples all the hair ridges start at the same point and come together again in the back while in others only the middle ridge is centered and the side ridges are roughly parallel" (1980:115). In some examples the high ridges cover only the central part of the crown, with low parallel rows along the sides, while in others the high ridges cover the entire crown. This high-ridged style is the one most frequently seen in Alldridge's photos.

That the high-ridged hairstyle had wide distribution in nineteenth-century sowei masks is suggested by the fact that it is the style represented on the first example of such a mask to be illustrated (Buttikoffer 1890, II:309). Johann Buttikoffer's discussion and illustration of a sowei mask is actually the first mention of the mask type. The mask that he collected (now in the Bernisches Historiches Museum) he found in the town of Tosso, in the Liberian Vai country, in November 1881 (fig. 33). Masks by the same carver were still found in Liberia at least as late as the 1960s, and the style was still being carved as late as the 1980s, though the hairstyle itself is regarded as old-fashioned and is no longer worn today.

In the Mende areas of Sierra Leone, Phillips found that while most of the masks with the high-ridged hairstyle dated from the turn of the century, some dated from as late as the 1930s. In addition, three recently carved masks were explicitly stated to have been exact copies of masks carved around the turn of the century (1980:115). Four other masks with a related style had "parallel ridges of hair of even height covering the whole scalp rather than the central portion alone" (ibid.:116). Phillips also noted that in the 1980s women could still occasionally be seen wearing this low-ridged variant.

A second group of masks depicts a hairstyle divided into four, six, or eight large lobes or 'buns' arranged around the crown of the head. Normally the lobes are then braided or tied together in a small knot at the top of the head, as seen in a photograph of a Mende woman from the turn of the century (fig. 34). Phillips's survey indicates that the four-lobed style was most common before World War I, and that since World War II the variations with six or eight lobes have been more popular (1980:116). These coiffures are often further elaborated by the addition of a plaited border at the hairline. This hairstyle is still occasionally worn by older women, and is one of the styles most likely to be worn by the elder heads of Sande.

Philllips names three further popular hairstyles. *Nyangabokui* gathers the hair

Fig. 33. *Sowei* mask,
Vai, Liberia. Drawing:
Büttikofer 1890: 309.

into many small buns that taper into little twists. *Ngovola* takes its name from the umbrella palm, whose spreading leaves it is thought to resemble. Another style named *Konro* consists of many small ball-like forms that cover the head, sometimes in combination with other forms, such as the ridged style. According to Phillips, this style is still worn by Mende women in the Kenema district of Sierra Leone (1980:117).

One other style deserves special mention: a number of masks illustrate a netlike form, usually in combination with the ridged hairstyle. This represents the practice of placing a net of black-dyed raffia or oil-palm fiber over the hair, not so much to control it as to augment it. Its representation on masks is far more common than its contemporary use, although women do add extensions to their hair today.

A mask's coiffure is often embellished with one or more additional carved elements, including amulets, cowrie shells, and animal horns. All of these are also occasionally added to a woman's coiffure, especially for occasions such as her return from the Sande initiation camp. The practice of braiding items into the hair was recorded by John Atkins as early as 1721 (1737:61). The amulets, known as *lasimoisia*, consist of Arabic script, usually passages from the Koran, enclosed in either a leather packet or a silver covering. Leather-covered lasimoisia are still frequently worn, but at the end of the nineteenth century Sande initiates returning from the bush more often wore silver-covered lasimoisia. Photographs of prominent women of the period illustrate how they too occasionally braided lasimoisia into their hair. Today, a Sande mask dancer normally has a *lasimoi* (singular) attached inside the mask or to her costume, for protection from evil spirits or jealous intentions. But the fact that lasimoisia are decorative as well as protective can be seen by the way they have been replaced in contemporary hairstyles by masses of safety pins, especially among girls returning from Sande initiation.

Sande-society masks often show lasimoisia in the hair. They also frequently show the use of animal horns, which have the same function as the amulets: the horns of antelope, duiker, goats, sheep, or even bush cows were traditionally filled with herbs for protection. Like the leather and silver amulets, these also serve to enhance the attractiveness of the mask. Cowrie shells, another motif frequently found on the masks, represent wealth.

Fig. 34. Portrait of a woman,
Mende, Sierra Leone, early 20th century.
Photo: Courtesy Brooklyn Museum of Art Library.

All of these features, as well as the incorporation of such unusual motifs as inverted cooking pots, birds, snakes, pigs, and chameleons, serve to embellish the masks and to make each one distinctive. For both the carvers who make the masks and the women who commission them, it matters that they be individually distinguished. The role of the mask as an archetype is central to its ceremonial importance, but the individuality of the mask is also important in identifying the particular town and chapter of the Sande society with which it is associated. In a sense, then, the individualization of the mask is parallel to the way women individualize themselves through the styling of their hair. The masks must conform to the stylistic canon while at the same time having an individual identity, as witnessed by their individual personal names.

While sowei masks are by far the most common sculptural form produced in the region, there are also a number of wooden female figures (cat. 92), most of them free-standing figures associated with medicine societies such as the Yassi and Humoi. They may also serve as prestige objects for chiefs and other high-ranking officials. Other figurative sculptures are incorporated on dance staffs, musical instruments, cosmetic pallets, or hammock suspension bars. The same treatments of hair seen on sowei masks are found on these pieces, by far the most common of them being the high-ridged style and the four-lobed style mentioned above. Probably 80 percent of these female figures wear the high-ridged hairstyle. In all cases, women are represented sculpturally without head ties.

Male figures are much more rare, and almost without exception depict men wearing hats. In contrast to the elaborate hairstyles of women, the men of the region traditionally keep their hair closely cropped. The earliest photographs, from the late nineteenth century, show that this was the pattern then as well. Even the earliest-known carvings from the region—the stone figures of the Sapi, believed to date from the sixteenth century or earlier—generally show men wearing hats of various types. Sapi figures of men without hats, identified as coming from the coastal areas, show closely cropped hairstyles with elaborately shaved geometric patterns; figures coming from the interior areas show men wearing plaited hairstyles. Dapper's account from the seventeenth century mentions the braiding of men's hair when they return from the Poro initiation camp (1668:414), and also in preparation of the body before burial (ibid.:403).

In contrast, Sapi female stone carvings, especially those from the northern region usually identified as 'Kissi,' frequently show elaborate hairstyles, most particularly the high-ridged type seen on early sowei masks. This suggests the intriguing possibility that at least some of the hairstyles seen in the region during the past century, and documented in photographs, may have a much greater antiquity, and that they have in fact been documented in sculpture for over 500 years. In any event, the representation of hairstyles on sculpture from this region is among the most detailed and realistic in any style region in Africa.

Cat. 92
Figure
Mende/Sherbro, Sierra Leone/Liberia
Wood. H: 33.5 cm.
Cecilia and Irwin Smiley

Coiffures of *the Dan* and *Wè* of Ivory Coast in 1938-1939

Elze BRUYNINX

In 1938-39, Pieter Jan Vandenhoute carried out research among the Dan and the Wè (Upper Cavally region) of Ivory Coast, during an expedition organized by the University of Gent and the Vleeshuismuseum, Antwerp. He is especially renowned for his study of Dan and Wè masks (Vandenhoute 1948). Apart from a large body of written materials, Vandenhoute also left a great number of photographs.

As Vandenhoute writes, "From the variety of coiffures two remarkable characteristics stand out among both sexes: first of all, the hair on top of the head is shaved, often neatly lined by means of a thin twilled ribbon … , so that it sits as high on the forehead as possible, which the Dan consider very beautiful and distinguished. The coiffure with braids along the cheeks, which is of typical Diomande origin, is also very common. Both characteristics are very strikingly represented in masks." (1945: XLVI-II–XLIX) (cat. 93). This also goes for the western Dan (of Liberia), studied by E. Fischer and H. Himmelheber, who write that "the forehead itself must be lined by a clearly rounded, evenly drawn, arched ring of hair. In order to achieve this effect, corrections are made by plucking or shaving single tufts of hair" (1976: 31).[1]

Vandenhoute's photographs show that the Dan and the Wè wore several different coiffures. Of the types that were fashionable among men, women, and children in 1938-39, we will mention just a few. From the hundreds of photographs Vandenhoute made, I have selected a picture of a bearded man from the Dan village of Glolé, who wears his hair short except in the middle of his head. Along the back and down to the neck runs a vertical strip of hair, tied with a piece of string that ends in two leopard's teeth joined together. The object serves as an amulet "to live a long life" (fig. 35).[2] Soothsayer-healers such as Nawluon Gweon, from the Wè village of Guedyi, wear flamboyant coiffures, with their hair shaved in dots and a thick braid that reaches down to the neck. Brass bells are attached to the head as embellishment, from which a tangle of woven and tied knots cascades onto the forehead (fig. 36).

The women too attach a great deal of importance to their coiffures, which can take different shapes, as with the men. Vandenhoute photographed one of the many

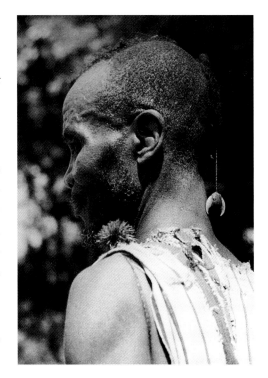

OPPOSITE
Cat. 93
Face mask
Dan, Côte d'Ivoire
Wood, fiber. H: 24.1 cm.
Saul and Marsha Stanoff

Fig. 35.
Bearded man from the Dan village of Glolé.
Photo: Vandenhoute, 1938–39, IV.F.II.20-8.

Fig. 36. Soothsayer healer, Nawluon Gweon, from the Wè village of Guedyi.
Photo: Vandenhoute, 1938–39, IV.F.IX. 159-8.

Fig. 37. One of the wives of the chief of Toulépleu.
Photo: Vandenhoute, 1938–39, IV.F.VII. 131-9.

Fig. 38. Woman of northern Wè origin at the market in the Dan village of Man.
Photo: Vandenhoute, 1938–39, IV.F.V. 86-8.

wives of the chief of Toulepleu, who shows us a coiffure that makes use of a pin. Her arched forehead is clearly lined by a delicate braid and the coiffure is further divided into lightly undulating lobes (fig. 37). Another picture, taken at the market in Man, in Dan territory, shows a woman of northern Wè origin (called Wobé in older literature) whose hair is parted down the middle, undulating down each side and ending in bulbs at the ears (fig. 38).

The variety of the coiffures is apparent once again in the picture of a woman and child from Biankuma (northern Dan). The woman's high forehead, lined with a braid, shows a crest that ends in a chignon at the neck. We can also see two braids at each side, between the ear and the cheek (fig. 39). The coiffure of the wife of the Niao chief at Ganya, in Wè-territory, is very artful: her high, arched forehead is lined with a series of braids that end in the neck, while the top of her head is covered with many separated braids that are interwoven at the back, creating an excellent chignon at the base of the neck. Two braids descend along her face (fig. 40, cat. 94).

The coiffures of babies, children, and teenagers show as much variety as those of men and women. In a photograph taken at Biankuma, for example, a Dan child on its mother's arm has short-trimmed hair but also a braid turned forward on top of its head (fig. 41). The forward braid is also found among adults. A young Dan at Flanpleu keeps his hair short except for the temples and the top of the head, where the hair forms a band. Some also have part of the back of the head shaved entirely except for a chignon (fig. 42). In the Dan village of Nuonleu, Vandenhoute saw two young children, one wearing his hair fairly high, the other with shaved temples and an arched strip of hair that reaches to his ears (fig. 43). At Toulépleu, Vandenhoute photographed two of the chief's children. One wears a fine forehead-braid, and the coiffure as a whole has a three-part structure. The taller child is already wearing an adult coiffure, braided in bands that come together at the back of the head. A braid noticeably sticks out in front (fig. 44).

However, from Vandenhoute's photograph archive and its accompanying notes,

Fig. 39. Woman with child from northern
Dan village of Biankuma.
Photo: Vandenhoute, 1938–39, IV.F.V. 89-10.

Fig. 40. Wife of the Niao chief at Ganya in
Wè territory.
Photo: Vandenhoute, 1938–39, IV.F.VII. 134-10.

Cat. 94
Figure
Dan, Côte d'Ivoire
Copper alloy. H: 22.5 cm.
Henau Collection, Antwerp

it seems apparent that there was little or no distinction between Dan and Wè hairstyles, that soothsayers wore their hair in complex shapes, and that the coiffures and headdresses of initiates were prescribed by certain guidelines. This has also been observed among the Dan from Matongwine. The initiates wore women's clothing in order to accentuate the transition from child to adult male (fig. 45). The braids along the cheeks were taken from the Diomande in the spirit of creativity. Standards of beauty among the Dan and Wè, as well as personal traits, undoubtedly also played a part in choosing a particular hairstyle.

Regarding other African cultures we know that certain coiffures are connected with or depend upon things like age, sex, or status. Magico-religious and other factors are also said to influence the hairstyles. Whether the coiffures that Vandenhoute photographed in 1938–39 were subject to particular guidelines is not entirely clear.

1. "Die Stirn selbst muss durch einen klar gerundeten, gleichmässig gezogenen bogenförmigen Haarkranz abgeschlossen sein. Hierzu werden am Haaransatz durch Auszupfen oder Rasieren einzelner Haarbüschel Korrekturen vorgenommen."

2. "Pour vivre longtemps." The IV.F. number refers to Vandenhoute's photo albums and to his accompanying notes.

OPPOSITE
Fig. 41. Dan woman and child in the village of Biankuma.
Photo: Vandenhoute, 1938–39, IV.F.VII. 117-12.

Fig. 42. Young Dan boy at Flanpleu.
Photo: Vandenhoute, 1938–39, IV.F.III. 48-7.

Fig. 43. Two young children in the Dan village of Nuonleu.
Photo: Vandenhoute, 1938–39, IV.F.II 27-10.

Fig. 44. Two children of the chief of Toulépleu.
Photo: Vandenhoute, 1938–39, IV.F.VII. 131-12.

Fig. 45. Young initiates in the Dan village of Matongwine.
Photo: Vandenhoute, 1938–39, IV.F.III. 55-4.

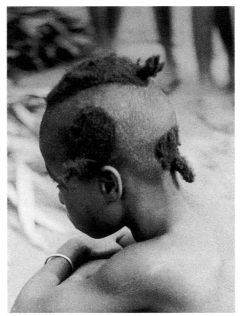

Fig. 46. Two Bayengi chiefs.
Photo: The Baptist Missionary Society,
early 20th century.

Children and Dolls

Infants and toddlers of both sexes have their head shaved except, in some
instances, for tufts of hair left to protect the fontanel. Girls receive, or make
for themselves, dolls that instruct them and at the same time insure their
adult responsibilities as mothers.

Ellis, writing of the Akan of what is now the country of Ghana in 1887,
reports that a girl in "announcing her eligibility for marriage . . . is carefully
adorned with all the ornaments and finery in the possession of the family,
and frequently with others borrowed for the occasion. . . . The hair is
covered with gold ornaments" (1887:235) (see fig. 51).

[R.S.]

Fig. 47. Mother and child,
Gciriku of the Kavango group, Namibia.
Photo: Anneliese Scherz, 1940s.

Fig. 48. Children with ostrich-eggshell
beads in their hair,
!Xu, Bushman (San), Namibia.
Photo: Anneliese Scherz, 1940s.

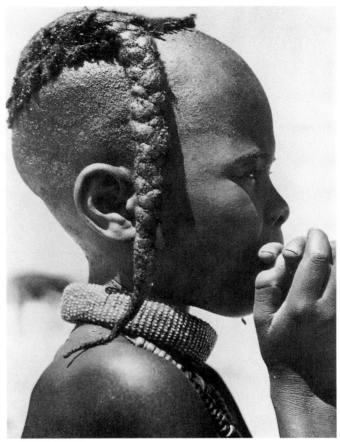

Fig. 49. Woman with doll, Bidjogo, Guinea.
Photo: Bernatzik, first half 20th century.

Fig. 50. Boy with plaits
(*ozondato* and *ondengura* neckband,
Himba, Namibia.
Photo: Anneliese Scherz, 1940s.

Fig. 51. Young women during
coming-of-age ceremonies,
Fanti, Ghana.
Photo: Roy Sieber, 1964.

Cat. 95
Fertility figure/doll
Mwali, Tonga/Yao, Zimbabwe
Calabash, sand, seeds. H: 22.9 cm.
Roy and Sophia Sieber

Cat. 96
Fertility figure
Ashanti, Ghana
Wood. H: 24 cm.
Henau Collection, Antwerp

Cat. 97
Figure
Bagirimi or Kenga, Chad
Wood, dark patina. H: 25.5 cm.
Cecilia and Irwin Smiley

Cat. 98
Fertility figure/doll
Bagarra, Sudan
Fiber, wood, metal, beads. H: 37 cm.
Private Collection, Belgium

A Note on Hair and Mourning Especially in Ghana

Roy SIEBER

Among many African peoples, shaving the head has been a primary symbol of mourning, although local variations exist. A tradition that Barrie Reynolds described for the peoples of the Gwembe Valley in Zambia may serve as typical:

> On the death of a parent, spouse or offspring, both sexes usually have their heads shaved as a sign of mourning. There is no ritual attached to the shaving which is performed by a close relative. The new growth of hair is allowed to grow undisturbed. The only exception is in the east, for the mother of the deceased. Through the secondary growth, a long furrow is cut from the peak of the forehead over the crown to the back of her head. A second furrow is made, roughly along the line of the suture between the frontal and parietal bones of the skull. These furrows are not renewed but are allowed to grow out with time (1968:195).

Across the continent, A.B. Ellis in 1887 described somewhat similar ceremonies observed at death among the Akan of Ghana:

> The nearest relations of the deceased of both sexes, shave the head and all hair from their bodies. This has commonly been regarded as a sign of grief; but having in view the shaving of the head by women on the sacred days of deities, which are days or rejoicing, it appears rather to be a sign of respect, or an offering—in the case of a death, art offering to the [soul] of the deceased (241).

Very few reports mention the disposition of the cut hair. However, there is evidence for the ritual treatment of cut hair among the peoples of southern Ghana. For example, Dennis M. Warren, in *The Akan of Ghana*, reports:

> Blood relatives shave and heap their hair at the house entrance; a great amount is an honour for the deceased. If the person had been very old, he and the living

Fig. 52. Bowl. Nsoko, Ghana. Copper alloy, 14th century (?).
Photo: Roy Sieber, 1964.

grandchildren were smeared with white clay (hyire), *a mark of victory for having lived long and produced many offspring. Today shaving of heads is often begged off by paying a small fee* (1973:20).

Among the best studies of the Asante are those of Captain R. S. Rattray. In *Religion and Art in Ashanti*, he reports that six days after burial,

> *A pot is now produced, the abusua kuruwa, i.e. the family pot. This pot general-ly has a lid or cover (fig. 53) which has been fashioned to represent the dead. . . . All the blood relations of the deceased now shave their heads; this hair is placed in the pot. About sundown some of the women of the clan take the whole of the utensils . . . [and] the food, and the "family pot" containing the hair . . . and pro-ceed, being very careful not to look behind them, to the "thicket of ghosts," i.e. the burial-ground, where all these articles are deposited, not on the grave, but in a part of cemetery known as* asensie, *"the place of the pots." Here the . . . cooking stones are set in position, the cooking pot placed upon them, . . . and "family pot" set down beside them; at the same time the following words are spoken:*

>> Here is food.

>> Here are (hairs from) our heads.

>> Accept them and go and keep them for us.

> *The path down which they have passed is closed by laying across it a creeper, at the same time speaking the following words:*

>> We have finished your funeral rites, ...

>> We have closed the path:

>> It is finished.

> *They then return to the spot where all the rest of the villagers are awaiting them* (1927:164–65).

At times the final, formal funeral might not take place for months, even years after death and burial. In those instances it was at the formal funeral that the abusua kuruwa was exhibited in a temporary shrine hut.

The city or Nsoko (Nsawkaw, Soko) in the Bron region of what is now western Ghana was once an important stop on a major trans-Saharan trade route. R. Austin Freeman visited the city in the 1890s.

> *In the evening of our arrival at Soku, while taking a tour of inspection of the town, I noticed in several of the streets piles of large stones placed against walls, the interstices of the stones being filled with hair, evidently human. I applied . . . for an explanation of the curious arrangement and [was] informed . . . that it was, as I had surmised, connected with religious beliefs of the district. When any native of the place . . . cut his hair, he carefully gathered up the cuttings and car-ried them to one of these cairns, where he deposited them, placing on top of them one of the stones, which being the property of the fetish could not be removed. He went on to point out the necessity for this observance. The cairns of sacred stones were simply a precaution against witchcraft, for if a man were not thus careful in disposing of his hair some of it might come into the possession of*

Fig. 53. Funerary vessel with 'portrait' head. The hairstyle is typical of a priest. Kwahu, Ghana.
Photo: Roy Sieber, 1964.

his enemies, who would, by means of it, be enabled to cast spells over him and thus compass his destruction (1899:171–72).

There were also reports of "bronze" basins in Nsoko. On visits in 1964 and again in 1967 I observed a pile of stones similar to the "cairns" reported by Freeman. However, the one I saw was topped with two copper-alloy (possibly bronze) basins. It was dedicated to the queenmother and was in a passageway opposite her shrine. The larger basin was clearly Mamluk (fourteenth century, Egyptian); the smaller, inside the larger, was of a type called *kuduo* (fig. 52). It appeared to be of later, local manufacture, although a copy of the Mamluk style. On my first visit a few traces of hair were present with a stone on top in the smaller vessel. On my second visit there was a great deal more hair, topped by the same stone and comparable to a 1980 photo by Raymond Silverman (1983:plate XXI). The bowl had suffered damage in the ensuing decade and a half, and had been separated from the larger bowl.

I was told (as others had been and later would be) that the hair was that from the shaved heads of relatives mourning the death of the queenmother. Clearly the shrine was a sacred site and the hair was as Freeman described, protected from evil-doers. It would seem that the accumulation of hair in 1967 and again in 1980 was the result of the deaths of two queenmothers.

There does seem to be a contextual parallel between the abusua kuruwa vessels of the Asante and the brass bowls of the Bono on the Nsoko shrine, although no direct connection has been established.

ORILONISE: The Hermeneutics of the Head and Hairstyles among the Yoruba

Babatunde LAWAL

The emphasis on the head (*Ori*) in Yoruba figure sculpture (cat. 99) goes beyond its biological importance as the seat of the brain, which controls the body. It also reveals the anthropocentric nature of Yoruba cosmology, which identifies the Supreme Being, Olodumare, as the head of a pantheon of deities called *orisa*, who act as the agents of its enabling power (*ase*). Hence the Supreme Being is sometimes called Oba Orun, the King of Heaven, and Olu Iwa, Lord/Head of Existence (Idowu 1995:37–38; and Euba 1985:3).[1]

> The Head should be accorded His due
> This is the oracle's charge to the one thousand seven hundred divinities
> Who must render annual tributes to Olodumare (Idowu 1995:53).

The supremacy of Olodumare is also reflected in the common sayings *Ori lo da ni, enikan o í d'Ori o* (It is the Head that created us; nobody created the Head) and *Ori eni, l'Eleda eni* (One's head is one's creator) (dos Santos and dos Santos 1971:49; see also Abiodun 1986:18). Be that as it may, the apical position of the physical head resonates in the traditional Yoruba system of government. For example, all members of an extended family living together are under the authority of a compound head (*Baálé ilé*), while all compound heads are responsible to a quarter head (*Olori adugbo*). Any matter that the latter could not resolve would be referred to a higher authority such as the village head (*Baálè* or *Olu*). At the top of this hierarchy is the Oba, a divine king, high priest, and the ruler of a given town, who is assisted by a council of elders or chiefs (Ojo 1966:119–20). Thus the head is to an individual what Olodumare is to the cosmos and a king to the body politic—a source of power.

In order to fully understand the significance of this metaphor, we must be aware of the Yoruba creation myth that traces the origin of the human body to an archetypal sculpture (*ere*) modeled by the artist-deity Obatala, after which it is activated by the divine breath (*emi*) of Olodumare, located in the sculpture's head. This creative

Cat. 99
Figure: *ibeji*
Yoruba, Nigeria
Wood. H: 26.7 cm.
Mr. and Mrs. Donald Morris

OPPOSITE
Cat. 100
Figure, mother and child
Yoruba, Nigeria
Wood. H: 42.5 cm.
Collection of Rita and John Grunwald

process occurs inside a pregnant woman's body and takes about nine months to mature. According to the myth, every individual, before being born into the physical world, must proceed to the workshop of Ajalamopin, the heavenly potter, to choose one out of several undifferentiated, ready-made *Ori Inu*, the "inner heads" on display in Ajalamopin's workshop. Each "inner head" contains Olodumare's ase (enabling power), and the one chosen by an individual predetermines his/her lot (*ipin*) in the physical world.[2] Hence the popular Yoruba slogan "*Orilonise*": One's success or failure in life depends on the head.[3]

Iconology of the Head

Yoruba religion focuses on the worship of the orisa because of the belief that they act on behalf of Olodumare, who is too exalted to be approached directly. Yet Olodumare is indirectly involved in the day-to-day life of an individual through his/her Ori Inu, which is also called *Ori Apere, Asiniwaye* (Venerable head, one's guardian spirit in the physical world) (Ladele et al. 1986:42). That is why, in the past, every adult Yoruba dedicated an altar to the Ori Inu. The practice continues today in the rural areas. Called *ibori*, the altar is a cone-shaped object containing divination powder (*iyerosun*) mixed with earth into which a diviner has chanted sacred incantations and verses meant to attract good luck to its owner (fig. 54). It is encased in leather and adorned with cowrie shells *(owo eyo)*. The ibori is kept in a crown-shaped container called *ile ori* (house of the head), which is lavishly embroidered with as many as 12,000 cowrie shells (fig. 55). The size and ornateness of the container depend on the social or economic status of its owner. It is to the ibori that an individual offers presents and prayers every morning before turning to the family orisa. This, again, underscores the preeminence of Olodumare, whom the inner head represents in an individual. Hence

Fig. 54. Altar for the "inner head" *(ibori)*. Mixed media. Obafemi Awolowo University Art Museum, Ile-Ife, Nigeria. *Photo: Babatunde Lawal, 1974.*

Fig. 55. House for the "inner head" *(ile ori)*, formerly owned by a king. Mixed media. Obafemi Awolowo University Art Museum, Ile-Ife, Nigeria. *Photo: Babatunde Lawal, 1974.*

Fig. 56. Second burial figure *(ako)*. Wood. Owo Museum, Owo, Nigeria. *Photo: Robin Poynor, 1973.*

the popular saying *"Ko s'orisa ti i da ni i gbe lehin ori eni"* (No orisa can help an individual without the consent of his or her head) (Abimbola 1971:81; see also Idowu 1995:38–56, Alade 1972:8–10, Lawal 1985, and Okemuyiwa and Fabunmi 1989:15–20). Moreover, the orisa themselves are said to be subject to their own Ori (Abimbola 1976:115), which means that, in spite of their popularity as the agents or manifestations of ase, they can assist a person only within the possibilities already predetermined by the Supreme Being, the Ultimate Head.

Although the physical head is highly valued because of its social and biological importance as a site of perception, communication, and identity, it is regarded as no more than the outer shell for the inner head. Hence it is called *Ori Ode* (External head). The desire for harmony between the two aspects of the head is expressed in the popular prayer *"Ori inu mi ko ma ba ti ode je"* (May my inner head not spoil my outer one) (Drewal, Pemberton, and Abiodun 1989:26). Consequently, the degree of realism in Yoruba portraiture depends on which aspect is being emphasized. Naturalism is favored in most of the sculptures meant to recall the physical likeness of an individual, such as the terra-cotta and bronze heads from Ife, as well as the *ako* second-burial effigies that mark the last symbolic appearance of a deceased ancestor among the living (fig. 56). On the other hand, sculptures placed on altars to communicate with the orisa or the spirits of dead ancestors are often stylized to emphasize their nonmaterial state of existence, even if they have a human essence.[4] Nonetheless, the importance of the head is apparent in both naturalistic and stylized representations, not only through its size but also through the detailed and elaborate treatment of the hairdo, which often rises like a crown, proclaiming the head's lordship over the body.

Art and Language of Yoruba Hairstyles

The Yoruba sometimes refer to *Homo sapiens* as *Eda, Omo Adáríhurun* ("Humanity, the species that grows hair mainly on the head"), partly because the human body is not covered with hair, like that of the lower animals, and partly because the hair that grows on the lower part of the abdomen is usually covered by dress. As a result, only the hair on the human head and face is noticeable. The hair on the head (*irun Orí*) is often likened to a grove that must be well maintained to hallow the sanctuary that the physical head constitutes for the Ori Inu, the inner head. That is why Yoruba women regard hairdressing as a mark of honor to the inner head, apart from its social significance (Araba 1978:8).

It will be recalled that the Yoruba creation myth identifies the human body as a work of art produced by the artist deity Obatala. One implication of the myth is that the human body encapsulates a special power (ase) that continually inspires and sustains the human "will to adorn," as well as the creativity manifest in the visual, performing, and applied arts, transforming much of what was once a wilderness into the civilization it is today (Lawal 1996:23–24). It is pertinent to note that the Yoruba word for civilization is *olaju*, which can be broken up etymologically as *o-la* = to cut, *oju* = face/head, that is, "to give the earth a human face."[5] In other words, the Yoruba have not only redesigned their habitat, they have personified the earth as a beauty-conscious goddess whose cognomen is *"Ile, Ogere, A f'oko yeri"* (Earth, the goddess who combs her hair with a hoe), an allusion to the farming and building activities that continually shape and reshape the human environment (Verger 1966:35, Adeoye 1989:359).

The earth, as a goddess, is thought to have two aspects, the hard (negative) and the soft (positive), represented by paired male and female figures respectively (Lawal 1995: 41–47). The village or town denotes the ordered, cultured, and predictable, and the jungle (igbo) the unordered, uncultivated, and unpredictable.[6] By the same token, a sloppily dressed person is ridiculed as *ara oko* (literally, "bush creature"), while unkempt hair is likened to a jungle and the individual concerned is easily mistaken for a psychopath. To be socially acceptable, therefore, is to be well groomed, paying special attention to one's behavior, clothes, and hair. This accounts for the emphasis on appearance in Yoruba culture. Besides, it is believed that taking good care of one's hair is an indirect way of currying favor with one's Ori Inu; as a result, the Yoruba have created a wide range of hairstyles that not only reflect the primacy of the head but also communicate taste, status, occupation, and power, both temporal and spiritual. The richness of the tradition can be gleaned from Yoruba masks and figure sculptures that will be used to illustrate the major styles, though they are often idealized in art for aesthetic reasons.

Children's Hair

In the past, the parents of a new baby often consulted a diviner on the third day after its birth to find out, among other things, the nature of the baby's inner head, and what should be done to preserve a good destiny or to rectify a bad one. This ceremony is called *imori* ("know the head") or *ikose waye* ("the first steps on earth") (Idowu 1995:192). To formally welcome the baby to the world of the living (*Ile Aye*), there is a naming ceremony on the seventh or ninth day after its birth during which its head is completely shaved.[7] Until the ceremony, the baby is often addressed as "*Omo titun, alejo aye*" (New baby, a stranger to the physical world). However, babies born with knotted or curly hair are considered sacred and are automatically given the name dada or ekine. Partly because they are thought to be special gifts from the orisa and partly because their knots of hair are likened to cowrie shells (money), these children are thought to attract wealth to their parents.[8] Hence Dada's panegyric (*oriki*):[9]

> *Dada Awuru...*
> *The one who wears a crown of money*
> *The one who wears an embroidered dress*
> *The one who carries a leaded staff of office*
> *You carry a big crown of money to the market [author's translation]* (Sowande and Ajanaku 1969:43).

Consequently, a dada's head is not shaved during the naming ceremonies, due to the belief that the knotted hair has special powers. The hair may be washed but must not be combed. As Marilyn Houlberg has noted, the "heads of dada children are shaved only under special ritual conditions. The act of head-shaving may be said to mark the incorporation of the already sacred child into the world of the living"

Fig. 57. Headdress for Egungun (ancestral) mask depicting the *aaso oluode* hairstyles worn by hunters and warriors. The two heads in the front wear the common *aaso oluode,* while the biggest one wears the longer variety that hangs down on the left side of the head. Wood. National Museum, Lagos, Nigeria.
Photo: Babatunde Lawal, 1995.

(Houlberg 1979:377). Like dada, twins (*ibeji*) are also regarded as sacred because of their unusual birth. As a result, their heads are usually not shaved during their naming ceremonies, this being done at a later date. In some areas of Yorubaland, especially among the Ijebu, the heads of twins are painted with special designs during the ritual that initiates them into the cult of twins (Adeoye 1979: 165-66).

As a male child grows older, the head is shaved clean (*irun fifa korodo*) about once a month or when it appears overgrown. Sometimes the back and sides of the head are shaved, leaving a strip of hair called *jongori* running from the front to the occiput. A patch of hair left on the crown is called *osu*. Young girls, on the other hand, are usually allowed to wear their hair long, though it is knotted or braided into designs similar to those worn by maidens and older women. Identical hairstyles easily identify a pair, male or female, as twins. By and large, parents endeavor to keep their children's hair as clean and decent as possible, because it is they who will be accused of negligence if a child's hair looks unkempt.

Young and Adult Males' Hair

Except for occupational or ritual reasons, most males shave their head, moustache, and chin until old age, when gray hair (*ewu*) and beard (*irugbon*) are considered marks of experience, wisdom, and maturity. Hence the popular saying "*Ewu l'ogbo, irungbon l'agba, mamu l'afojudi*" (Gray hair bespeaks old age, the beard bespeaks maturity, the moustache betrays insolence). Certain hairstyles, however, may indicate social status or unusual power. For example, instead of sporting the common *jongori* (the strip of hair in the middle of the head that runs from the front to the back), young princes as well the children of the rich may wear the *àáso*, which consists of three round patches of hair arranged in the front, center, and back of the head. Another variation of the *àáso* identifies powerful hunters and warriors, especially the *eso* (leaders of the military guards) (Adeoye 1989:164). Called *àáso oluode*, it is a patch of hair growing on a spot in the middle of the head into which potent medicine has been infused to empower the body both physically and spiritually. More often, this patch of hair is braided into a knot (fig.57), and may be made to hang down on the left side of the head (cat. 101). In order to accommodate the hair, some hunters and warriors wear a long, pouchlike cap called *adiro*, which is also used to store small charms. As a result, the cap hangs heavily on the left side of the head, almost touching the shoulder (for illustration see Picton 1994:fig. 1.3). Another peculiar male hairstyle, called *ifari apakan* because it leaves the head half-shaved, identifies an individual as a member of the Aragberi clan, a branch of the Aresa royal house of the Old Oyo empire whose leaders were noted for their deep knowledge of herbal medicine and magical charms (Adeoye 1979: 165–66).

Young and Adult Females' Hair

While most males shave their head, the females, young and old, are expected to keep their hair very long. The head of a female initiate or patient, however, may be shaved to allow special ingredients to be rubbed or incised onto the scalp. Otherwise, a majority of Yoruba women fashion their hair into assorted, crownlike designs (sometimes adorned with colorful beads) both to honor their inner head and in keeping

Cat. 101
Slit drum
Yoruba, Nigeria
Wood. H: 72 cm.
Rolf and Christina Miehler

Fig. 58.
Sango priestess wearing the
suku hairstyle, Oyo, Nigeria.
Photo: Robert Farris Thompson, 1964.

with the popular adage *"Irun l'ewa obinrin"* (The hair adds to a woman's beauty). There are three principal methods of shaping the hair: (a) loose weave (*irun biba*), a casual and temporary parting and knotting into big buns or cornrows until the styling can be done by a professional; (b) tight weave (*irun didi*), a detailed plaiting of the hair into intricate designs; and (c) binding (*irun kiko*), using a black thread to tie strands of hair into filaments that are then gathered to form intricate designs (Daramola and Jeje 1975:90).[10]

Being a temporary measure, the loose weave (irun biba) is usually covered with a scarf or head tie, although it may be left uncovered indoors. Since hair binding (irun kiko) is a relatively recent development, it will be discussed below in the section dealing with contemporary developments. In this section, I will focus on the tight weave or braid (irun didi), but space limitations will not allow a description of all the varieties; only the most popular ones will be highlighted.

The style in fig. 58, cat. 102 is called *suku* ("knotted hair"), because all the braids terminate in a short or long knot (suku) on the crown or back of the head. Fig. 59 is known as *kolese* ("without legs"), because all the braids start in the front and terminate separately or in a knot at the back of the head, very close to the neck. With the *ipako elede* ("pig's occiput") style, all the braids start from the back, terminating in rolls in front of the head (fig. 60). In the *panumo* ("close your mouth") style, one set of braids starts from the back and another set from the front, both terminating separately and leaving a gap in the middle of the head (fig. 62). A variation of this design shows braids starting from both sides of the head and terminating in scrolls on top of the head, leaving a gap in the middle of the head (fig. 61). In the style called *ojompeti* (rain falling on the ears), braids of various sizes run across the head, ending in small rolls or knots near the ears (cats. 103, 104). To create the *koroba* ("bucket") style, all the braids radiate from a point on the occiput, terminating in the front, sides, and back of the head and enclosing it like a vessel (fig. 70). In the *agogo* (cockscomb), one of the most conspicuous Yoruba hairstyles (fig. 63, cats. 100, 105, 106, 108, 109), the hair is parted into three sections, two on the sides of the head and one in the center; the side braids are in low relief, while the central one forms a crest that runs from the back to the front of the head. Sometimes the hair is parted into front, middle, and back sections, so that the central crest runs laterally from ear to ear, as in the ojompeti style.

In the past, one could easily tell from a woman's hairstyle whether or not she was married. Spinsters wore simpler forms of the ojompeti, ipako elede, or koroba styles. Brides and housewives, on the other hand, sported more intricate versions of the agogo and panumo styles. Wives of kings (olori) frequently distinguished themselves in public with elaborate versions of the suku style with a long knot in the middle of the head (see Johnson 1921:101, 125, Talbot 1926:412, and Houlberg

Fig. 59. *Kolese* hairstyle.
Drawing by Babatunde Lawal.

Fig. 60. *Ipako Elede* hairstyle.
Drawing by Babatunde Lawal.

Fig. 61. A variation of the *panumo* hairstyle. Drawing by Babatunde Lawal.

ABOVE
Fig. 62. Gelede headdress with *panumo* hairstyle.
Wood. National Museum, Lagos, Nigeria.
Photo: Frank Speed, 1971.

Cat. 102
Figures: *ibeji*
Yoruba, Nigeria
Wood. H: 29.2 and 28.6 cm.
Mr. and Mrs. Donald Morris

Cat. 103
Figures: *ibeji*
Yoruba, Nigeria
Wood. H: 26.7 and 26 cm.
Mr. and Mrs. Donald Morris

Cat. 104
Figure: *ibeji*
Yoruba, Nigeria
Wood. H: 19 cm.
Mr. and Mrs. Donald Morris

Cat. 105
Figure: *ibeji*
Yoruba, Nigeria
Wood. H: 22.9 cm.
Mr. and Mrs. Donald Morris

Fig. 63. Osun priest with the *agogo*
hairstyle, Osogbo, Nigeria.
Photo: Babatunde Lawal, 1972.

OPPOSITE
Cat. 106
Helmet Mask
Epa/Elefon, Yoruba, Nigeria
Wood. H: 96 cm.
Corice and Armand P. Arman

1979:368–69). Since these hairstyles can be found practically all over Yoruba country, it is difficult to discuss them strictly in terms of regional emphasis. Nonetheless, a particular style may be more popular in one area than another. For example, the agogo style is more popular in northern Yorubaland, especially among the Oyo. As a result, some scholars have suggested that the Oyo might have adapted the style along with others from the Fulani or Hausa, among whom it is also popular, and with whom the Oyo have had several centuries of cultural exchanges (Ladele 1986:203). Women in the coastal area, especially in the Ijebu-speaking towns, were in the past fond of dividing their hair into two parts or more and braiding them into hornlike projections (Johnson 1921:101, Talbot 1926:412). In eastern Yorubaland, especially at Owo, the women sometimes divide their hair into three or more large buns arranged in front of the head like a coronet. On ceremonial or ritual occasions, the buns may be adorned with small combs, beads, or the red tail-feather of the parrot (for illustration see Abiodun 1989:94, plate 94).

In general, a woman's hair may reflect her state of mind or important phases in her life, such as the naming ceremony of a new child, chieftaincy installations, marriage, and the various festivals in honor of the orisa. In the past, a widow was required to undo her braids, leave her hair disheveled, and remain indoors until the completion of her husband's funeral rites, which may last about three months. At the end of the mourning period, her head would be shaved clean to mark a symbolic separation from her deceased husband and a return to normal life (Daramola and Jeje 1975:153. Although Yoruba burial customs vary from area to area, in most cases the head of the corpse, male or female, was shaved clean before burial.

Hair, Religion, and Spirituality

Yoruba religion is organized into a number of cults, each with distinct artistic symbols, shrines, and priests dedicated to a particular orisa. Membership of a given cult is determined by a number of factors, such as being born into a priest's family, being fascinated with its public ceremonies, or because of the high reputation enjoyed by an orisa for solving personal problems ranging from impotence, infertility, and chronic illness to recurrent misfortunes. The initiation of a priest involves the shaving and treatment of the head with herbal preparations that sensitize it to the signals from the orisa. Henceforth, the individual must not carry a load on the head except objects sacred to the orisa. Frequently, a round patch of hair (osu) is allowed to grow in the center or front part of the head (cat. 107). But more often the head is left unshaved and then braided, regardless of sex. Esu priests wear their osu like a pigtail, called erè, which characterizes many Esu staff figures (fig. 64, cat. 110).

There is a special category of male and female priests who serve as spirit mediums for certain orisa such as Sango (thunder) and Soponna (smallpox). The female body is said to be ideal for this phenomenon, essentially because of the resilience that allows it to bear children without serious injury. Thus the initiation process metaphorically converts a male priest's body into a female's, to facilitate the manifestation of the orisa in it during possession. That is why both male and female priests are called iyawo. Although this term means "wife" in ordinary usage, it has no sexual implication but merely identifies the priest as a special confidant who ensures

Fig. 64. Esu figure with *ere* (pigtail) hairstyle, note the snail shell, *okoto*. Wood. National Museum, Lagos, Nigeria.
Photo: Babatunde Lawal, 1995.

Cat. 107
Divination bowl: *agere Ifa*
Yoruba, Nigeria
Wood. H: 24.1 cm.
Thomas D. Slater
The female figure wears a decorative hair attachment shaped like a tassel. The kneeling pose identifies her as a suppli-cant or a devotee of Orunmila (divination deity). The child on her back sports two braided *osu*, suggesting either that it was born through the intercession of the deity or had been initiated into its cult.

Cat. 108
Figure
Yoruba, Nigeria
Wood. H: 57 cm.
Rolf and Christina Miehler

Cat. 109
Figures: *ibeji*
Yoruba, Nigeria
Wood. H: 22.2 and 24.5 cm.
Donald Morris Gallery

Cat. 110
Fly whisk handle
Yoruba, Nigeria
Ivory. H: 11.5 cm.
Alan Brandt Inc.

Fig. 65. *Bayanni* cowrie-embroidered
crown sometimes worn by Sango priests.
Mixed media. Obafemi Awolowo
University Art Museum, Ile-Ife, Nigeria.
Photo: Babatunde Lawal, 1974.

a regular offering of sacrifices to an orisa in much the same way that a beloved wife caters to her husband. This is one of the reasons why such priests wear patently female hairstyles such as the *agogo, suku, koroba,* and *kolese* (see cat. 102, and fig. 59). To reinforce the "priest/wife" metaphor, male Sango priests often wear a *bante* (long skirt) that is essentially an elaborate form of a female *tobi* (underwear).

Of course the female hairstyle has an aesthetic significance as well. For example, the Yoruba word for possession is *gun,* meaning "to ascend," indicating that an orisa is figuratively "enthroned" on a priest's head, transforming it into a crown (*ade*). This imagery is evident in the beaded fringes attached to an Osun priestess's suku hairstyle, which recall a king's crown (for illustrations see Apter 1992:plates 5 and 7). Also crownlike is a special cowrie-embroidered headgear with veil, called *bayanni* (fig. 65), worn by Sango priests—sometimes replaced by a beaded hat with fringes—which identifies them, when possessed, as Sango incarnate (for illustration see Drewal and Mason 1998: plate 55). However, it should be emphasized that the female hairstyle does not always transform a male priest into a "wife." Neither is it confined to possession priests.[11] From the different interpretations that I collected in the field, it is apparent that cross-dressing in Yoruba religion has multiple, although related, layers of meaning. According to some informants, cross-dressing attempts to harness the spiritual dynamics that abide in male-female complementarity, a phenomenon also apparent in the pairing of male-female figures in Esu, Ifa, Ogboni, and Oro ritual symbols (see Lawal 1995).

Although not subject to possession as a professional priest is, the Oba is viewed as a living embodiment of Oduduwa, who is widely regarded as the progenitor of the Yoruba and the founder of divine kingship at Ile-Ife. Hence, during the installation rites, the head of a new king is shaved and washed with spiritual ingredients. Thereafter the king must not place anything on his head except the crown, whose conical form recalls both the ibori (see fig. 54) and the suku hairstyle worn by some orisa priests, emphasizing the king's dual role as ruler and the nominal head of all the orisa cults in his domain. No wonder some kings wore a patch of hair on the head, like an ordinary priest (Euba 1985:8). A female presence is suggested by the bird motif on the crown. Although this motif is commonly associated with ase in Yoruba iconography, and identifies the king as the wielder of a special ase, it also alludes to the mystical powers of women, which the king is expected to harness for the public good (see Thompson 1972:253–54 and Babayemi 1986:13). In the past, a king seldom appeared in public; but when he did, his face was partly concealed by the crown. However, there are some exceptions to this convention. At Owo, for example, the king (Olowo) appears in public with his face uncovered during the annual Igogo festival in memory of an ancient queen, Oronse, who disappeared under mysterious circumstances, leaving her head tie behind. So the wearing of hat or head tie is forbidden in the town during the Igogo festival. The king appears in public with his hair braided and adorned with the red parrot tail-feathers (fig. 66) (for illustrations see Drewal, Pemberton, and Abiodun 1989:17, plate 4, and Poynor 1995:34).

Lastly, since masks and altar sculptures mediate between the human and the spirit worlds, they are usually adorned with the priestly hairstyles favored by a given orisa cult. However, the hairstyle on a given figure or mask is normally determined by the carver, who has discretion over bodily details unless given specific instructions by a client. Statuettes dedicated to deceased twins (*ere ibeji*) also display priestly hairstyles, partly to honor the departed soul and partly to reflect the popular belief that the souls of twins run errands for the orisa, most especially for Sango, the thunder deity.

Hair, Politics, and Power

Such is the importance of hair in Yoruba religion that it is also used to reinforce political power. In many parts of Yorubaland, the messengers of the king (*oba*) sport special hairstyles to identify them in public. The messengers are recognized by their half-shaved heads (ifari apakan).[12] They are easily confused with members of the Aragberi clan, who wear a similar style—except that the latter may put on hats, if they choose to, whereas the royal messengers must leave their heads uncovered when on duty, to ensure instant public recognition.

A royal messenger (*ilari*) usually undergoes a special ritual during which his head is infused with charms to ensure his loyalty, to give him the confidence and courage to carry out the king's order, and to instill in the public, on seeing any of the king's messengers, the fear of his sacred power. After the ritual, the hair is allowed to grow, before one side is shaved clean. Nonetheless, there are regional variations in the hairstyle. In most of southwestern and eastern Yorubaland, the royal messengers simply shave half of the head (sometimes alternately) every cycle of four days (which constitutes the Yoruba week). At Ila-Orangun, court messengers wear only a round patch on the crown of a clean-shaven head (Houlberg 1979:373, plate 23). In northern Yorubaland, especially in Oyo, the cultural center of this area, the messenger's head is normally shaved alternately every fifth day, leaving a circular patch on the crown that is allowed to grow long, dyed with indigo, and braided into a crest (fig. 67) (Johnson 1921:62). But in Iganna, to the southwest of Oyo, the ilari sometimes wear the braid in the middle of the head (fig. 68).

It is important to note the similarities between Esu (the divine messenger) and the ilari or *emese* (another term for the royal messenger).[13] First, Esu altar figures are sometimes adorned with a cap with a different color on each side (illustrated in Pemberton 1975:20–27), recalling the half-shaved head of royal messengers. Some Esu priests wear the same hairstyle. This two-sided motif epitomizes the liminal status of the messenger as a catalytic agent of ase. Second, note the parallel between the pigtail or vertical, phallic hair of many Esu staff figures and the braided crest of some royal messengers (compare figs. 64 and 67). Both projections allude to higher powers from above. On the one hand Esu mediates between humanity and the orisa, and between the orisa and Olodumare. On the other, the court messenger links the Oba and his subjects, and one kingdom with another. So it was that, in precolonial times, royal messengers played crucial roles in Yoruba politics, not only because of the absolute loyalty that the initiation rituals demanded of them, but also because their peculiar hairstyles

Fig. 66. The Olowo of Owo with braided hair during the *Igogo* Festival, Nigeria.
Photo: Robin Poynor, 1973.

Fig. 67. Royal messengers *(ilari)* from Oyo, Nigeria, 1950s.
Photo: Pierre Verger.

Fig. 68. Gelede headdress with *ifari-apakan* combined with *osu* hairstyles. Wood. National Museum, Lagos, Nigeria. *Photo: Frank Speed, 1971.*

Fig. 69. Contemporary female hairstyle called "Eko Bridge," a curvilinear network of bridges in Lagos. Drawing by Babatunde Lawal.

gave them some measure of diplomatic immunity. To assault or kill a royal messenger was a tacit declaration of war on the kingdom he or she represented.

That was why, in the heyday of the Old Oyo empire, between the late seventeenth and early nineteenth centuries, court messengers served as the king's bodyguards, intelligence officers, land arbitrators, and ambassadors to vassal states (Olaniyan 1975:305–6). Each ilari had a special name, which expressed either the divine power of the king or his intention or disposition on a particular issue. In effect, the mere announcement of a messenger's name automatically delivered the gist of the message, so that the ilari's hairstyle served as a prima facie emblem of authenticity. However, some ilari were required to carry a staff of office (usually a beaded staff surmounted by a bird or equestrian figure motif) when going on important interstate missions, or when representing the king at coronation ceremonies in other parts of the Old Oyo empire and beyond.[14] The use of the beaded staff to authenticate royal messages continues in different parts of Yorubaland, even in areas where the messengers no longer wear special hairstyles.

Contemporary Developments

Although active worship of the inner head (Ori Inu), and related art forms, have declined in recent years due to the negative impact of Islam, Christianity, and Westernization, the belief that the inner head determines one's fortunes in life has not been totally abandoned. In fact, the enormity of the problems of survival in the modern era is such that Yoruba converts to Islam and Christianity—literate and non-literate—often fall back on the indigenous methods of managing stress. Many still patronize herbalists, diviners, and soothsayers in times of crisis, especially after all the newly introduced Western remedies have failed (see Dopamu 1979:3–20 and Abimbola 1991:51–58). Prayers in churches and mosques still recognize the important role that the inner head can play in helping an individual negotiate the complexity and competitiveness of modern living. The contemporary Yoruba musician Sunny Ade sums up the situation in this popular song released in 1982:

> *My head, please, fight for me, my spirit, please fight, fight for me*
> *My father's head, fight, fight for me, my mother's head, fight, fight for me*
> *Because the Blue Touraco's head fights for the Blue Touraco, the head of the*
> *Aluko bird fights, oh. . . .*
> *My Creator, don't forget me, please, it is better that you fight, oh*
> *(Waterman 1990: 144).*

The emphasis on the head continues in contemporary Yoruba art, though its forms, functions, and contexts are changing. The introduction of Western hairdressing tools, techniques, and materials at the beginning of the twentieth century, coupled with the influence of the mass media, has encouraged the adoption of foreign hairstyles, which now exist side-by-side with the indigenous ones—all reflecting the dynamics of change in Yorubaland. The availability of scissors and hand clippers (manual and electric) now makes it possible for a male to have his hair cut down and shaped into various styles, instead of the clean or partial shave necessitated by the use of razors during the precolonial era. Professional barbers now post assorted designs for the customer to choose from. Most of the new designs are made by commercial artists who copy them from foreign publications, especially fashion magazines (fig. 69). Each style has a name that either describes itself, such as "cockscomb," or conjures up the exotic, such as "San Francisco" or "Oklahoma." In some cases the name may identify the celebrity who initiated or popularized a given style. For instance, the low cut called "Joe Louis" was very popular in the 1940s because it was the trademark of the then reigning world heavyweight boxing champion. The styles in vogue between the 1950s and the 1970s included "Elvis Presley," "John Kennedy," "James Brown," and "Afro." Since then, other styles have been added, some influenced by local celebrities and topical events. They include *"udoji"* (commemorating the huge salary increase for Nigerian workers in the 1970s), *"bon-sue"* and *"na-poi"* (popular dance styles from Ghana), and *"apola"* (giant size). A recent influence from Jamaica's Rastafarian movement has led some young men and women to wear the dreadlocks and matted hair popularized by reggae music superstars such as the late Bob Marley—a phenomenon previously associated with dada children. Now it is difficult to tell who is a real dada!

Although the traditional hairstyles continue to enjoy popularity among the generality of Yoruba women, Western influences crept in during the colonial period (c. 1900–1960), when many educated ladies shampooed or stretched their hair in imitation of fashionable female hairdos in the West. In the 1960s and 1970s, wigs of

Fig. 70. *Gelede* headdress with *koroba* hairstyle. Wood. National Museum, Lagos, Nigeria.
Photo: Frank Speed, 1971.

assorted designs, especially the Afro, imported from the United States, became fashionable. The crude-oil boom in Nigeria in the 1970s and early 1980s stimulated a lot of economic, industrial, cultural, and artistic development all over the country. In Yorubaland it inspired new female hairstyles characterized by the use of black thread (*owu dudu*) to create intricate and high-rising coils and arches that evoke the social mood and landmarks of the period. Created by commercial artists, each design had a name, such as "Eko Bridge" (a curvilinear network of bridges in Lagos; see fig. 69), "Cocoa House" (a skyscraper in Ibadan), "Stadium" (the National Stadium, Lagos), "high profile" (social visibility), "udoji" (salary increase for workers), and "FESTAC" (National Theatre, Lagos).[15] The publication of these styles in pamphlet forms has not only helped to standardize some of the designs, it has also facilitated their diffusion to other parts of Africa, the Caribbean, the United States, and Brazil.

Making a Headway

In view of the common saying *Ori buruku ko gbose; Ayanmo o gbogun* ("A bad head cannot be washed clean with magical soap; destiny cannot be altered with charms"), one might be led to assume that an individual is powerless against the fate supposedly assigned to him or her before birth. Yet a close reading of the Yoruba notion of the inner head reveals the contrary. According to a divination verse, *Iwa nikan l'o soro; Ori kan kii buru l'Otu Ife* (It is character that matters; there is no recognizably bad head in Otu-Ife city) (Idowu 1995:161). A popular adage puts it differently: *Eni l'ori rere ti ko n'iwa, iwa l'o ma ba ori re je* (Even if someone is born with a good head, but lacks good character, this shortcoming will spoil his or her good head) (Fajana 1966:25; see also Lawal 1974:241). In other words, since all the inner heads made by the heavenly potter Ajalamopin look alike, and since one's destiny is concealed, it is difficult to differentiate a good head from a bad one. So one should struggle in life to improve one's worth and character. One Yoruba proverb puts it succinctly: *Owo ara eni l'a fi i tun iwa eni se* (It is up to an individual to make the best of his or her existence and character) (Ajibola 1978:31). A similar message is evident in the emphasis on the head in Yoruba art, since making headway in life depends, for the most part, on how well you utilize your head:

If I have money

It is my Ori [Head] I will praise

My Ori, it is you

If I have children on earth

It is my Ori to whom I will give praise

My Ori, it is you

All the good things I have on earth

It is Ori I will praise

My Ori, it is you (Abimbola 1976:133–34).

So it is that both the traditional and contemporary Yoruba hairstyles, along with various headgears, glorify the head, not only to enhance appearance and reinforce identity but to acknowledge the vital role the head plays in the quest for a successful life.

1. The Yoruba word *olu* (lord), a synonym for "head," is a title borne by the governors of small Yoruba towns. Hence some Yoruba translate *Oluwa*, another name for the Supreme Being, as "Our Overall Head." See Mustapha, Ajayi, and Amoo 1986:14.
2. Since the Yoruba word for fate is *ipin*; Ajalamopin means "Ajala, the molder of heads concealing a person's fate." Ajalamopin is also known as Ajala Alamo, "Ajala, the potter."
3. *Orilonise* is an abbreviation of the saying "*Orilonise, Eda Layanmo*" (The head determines one's lot in life; human potentials are predetermined).
4. For more on this, see Cordwell 1953:220–25, Abiodun 1976, and Lawal 1977: 50–61.
5. For other implications of the face in Yoruba art, see Lawal 1985:100–101.
6. A similar town/jungle, wilderness/civilization dichotomy has been noted in other African cultures. See, for instance, Vogel 1997:46.
7. Generally, a baby girl is named on the seventh day, a baby boy on the ninth day. There are some variations, however. In Ile-Ife, for instance, a girl is named on the sixth day and a boy on the seventh day. See Bascom 1969:56.
8. For more on this category of children, see Sowande and Ajanaku 1969:43–44, Houlberg 1979:375–78, and Drewal, Pemberton, and Abiodun 1989:26.
9. The literal translation of the term *oriki* is "head-praise." It is a chant addressed to the "Inner head" (*Ori Inu*) of a person, and is meant to inspire that person to live up to expectations.
10. Hair binding with thread (*irun kiko*) is also known as *irun olowu* (binding with thread).
11. The female hairstyle is also common among the priests of *Orisa Agemo* (associated with the spiritual well-being of the Ijebu Yoruba), who are not normally possessed by the orisa. See Margaret T. Drewal 1992:131–32, plates 7.2 and 7.3.
12. At Ijebu Ode, the royal messengers are called *odi*.
13. For a detailed analysis of these similarities, see Houlberg 1979:382–91.
14. According to Johnson 1921:468, Obakosetan, one of the Oyo king's senior *ilari*, carried as his staff of office a leather fan with red and green embroidery.
15. The National Theatre in Iganmu, Lagos, was specially constructed to host FESTAC, the "Second World Festival of Black Arts and Culture" held in Nigeria in February 1977. For illustrations of some of these hairstyles see Akinnuoye (n.d.); for an excellent analysis of some of them see Houlberg 1979.

Hair Style among
the Margi

James H. VAUGHAN

Hairstyle is important in all societies; it may be indicative of ethnic, class, or gender identity. This was memorably impressed upon me many years ago as I showed slides taken in 1959 or 1960 during my first period of fieldwork among the Margi of the Mandara Mountains of Nigeria. The Margi were then far less acculturated than they are today, and the people in my photographs appeared very exotic by current standards. My audience was composed of sophisticated, well-educated Americans, and they had correctly deduced from the slides that older Margi adults, both male and female, periodically shaved their heads and wore closely cropped hair. As I showed a slide of one of my female friends, I noticed two women in the audience whispering, and then one asked, "With the shaved heads, how can you tell the men from the women?" She asked this despite the fact that the woman in the slide was completely bare breasted. Clearly hairstyle was a more prominent gender marker than some more-obvious anatomical evidence. At that time American men and women commonly wore markedly different hairstyles. Only a few years later, our society was riven by disputes about the length of men's hair.

Today, as African states strive to integrate their populations, there is a tendency to affect styles that emphasize national and regional—even pan-African—identities. This has not always been the case, however. Formerly, it was not uncommon to find as many as a dozen societies, speaking distinct languages and having distinctive customs, in an area no larger than a mid-sized U.S. state. This was the case in the Mandara Mountains, where disparate societies found it important to differentiate themselves from their neighbors. Under those circumstances, visual markers that socially identified an individual not only were of practical value but were sources of cultural pride. Clothing was the most significant such marker, but another—particularly among women—was hairstyle. (It might also be noted that cultural identity was not so strong as to prevent different villages within a society from affecting their own styles—particularly a unique hairstyle.) In the Mandaras in the 1960s, the regional markets revealed a plethora of cultural differences, and it was among women that

OPPOSITE
Fig. 71. Mother and her one-week old daughter on the day of the infant's first showing. Both are covered in red ochre and the child's head has been shaved leaving a small central patch. Mandara Mountains, Nigeria.
Photo: James H. Vaughan, 1960.

one saw the most striking markers. Far more than men, women bore the visual hallmarks of their societies and their villages.

In a socially heterogeneous area like the Mandara Mountains, markets were true multicultural affairs where members of the various societies converged for activities both economic and social. For youths it was the latter that were of critical importance: not only did young people dress and coiff so as to say who they were ethnically, they were arrayed in order to attract the attention of members of the opposite sex. Hairstyle was a prominent item in the inventory of young Margi females, who took enormous pride in their coiffure. It would be incorrect, however, to think that there was a single hairstyle characterizing Margi women, for styles varied from village to village and from time to time. Yet everyone knew the "catalogue" and drew the correct conclusions. An eye-catching appearance was a matter of concern to youths of both sexes trying to appear attractive according to the conventions of the day. Furthermore, because of the heterogeneity of the markets, there was in these places a lack of the restraints that characterized daily village life. Under these more open circumstances, connections of family and village were less relevant, and more ephemeral criteria such as appearance became more important. Consequently, youths at markets often engaged in the kind of adolescent heterosexual display that we would find familiar, and this led to predictable results. Although first marriages among the Margi of that time were ordinarily arranged by the families of the couple, at the markets youthful indiscretions were, if not common, at least not uncommon. (I well remember the scandal that erupted in our village when, on one market day, one of our girls, despite being betrothed to a young man of her father's choosing, eloped with another with whom she had formed an attachment based on the openness of market days.)

The hairstyles of the Margi of that period may be generally differentiated in terms of gender and life-cycle. Children of both sexes characteristically had their heads periodically shaved; a few mothers would shave their infants' heads in such a way as to leave a distinctively shaped patch of hair. (Incidentally, one of the most striking characteristics of new Margi mothers was that they covered themselves, including their hair, with a mixture of red ocher and oil [fig. 71].) Males beyond childhood shaved their heads whenever their hair became much longer than an inch. (The only exceptions were the rulers of the several Margi kingdoms, who wore hair locks that they kept covered on all public occasions but for one annual ritual.) Females, on the other hand, went through two stages of hairstyle. From approximately the age of puberty, perhaps like youths the world over, young Margi women were very conscious of their appearance and in particular of their hair. During this period they wore elaborate, consciously chosen hairstyles that they often changed. Later, like the men, they shaved their heads with small wrought-iron blades whenever their hair got much longer than an inch. (The

Fig. 72. A particularly attractive young mother with a "Kanuri style" hairdo. Note that this child also has a hair patch.
Photo: James H. Vaughan, 1960.

mother in fig. 71 is wearing her hair at about its maximum length for this style.) There was no rule as to when women lost interest in more-elaborate hairstyles, but it would not be far amiss to say that it came after the birth of the first child or children, a time when other matters assume a greater importance in women's lives.

One of the most popular celebrations among Margi came some two to three months after the birth of twins. Like other Africans, the Margi have a very high incidence of twins. This celebration was called *ful bili*, or "twins' dance." People from surrounding villages would converge upon the home village of the new twins for a day-long festival. The most popular feature of the celebration was an ensemble dance by girls from the host village and, in the case of the ful

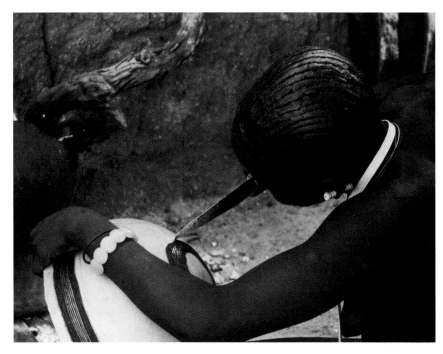

Fig. 73. A young woman burning decorations into a calabash. Her hair is arranged in parallel rows and covered with black oil.
Photo: James H. Vaughan, 1960.

bili of an important family, from surrounding villages as well. These girls would make elaborate preparations in secret during the days leading up to the festival. They would develop special clothing—an elaboration of their ordinary dress—and in particular they would affect a new hairstyle. (It should be added that this hairstyle often then became the mode until the next fad.) At the height of the afternoon's festivities, dancers from each of the participating villages were led by their drummers into the central court. Each group had its own clothing and hairstyle, and each tried to dazzle the crowd with its adornments and to outshine the participants from other villages. Each village took pride in the appearance of its young women, and as the women danced men often showed approval by tucking paper currency in their headbands. On one such occasion in 1960, the girls from my village affected a hairstyle that was then characteristic of women of the Kanuri, a large society in northeastern Nigeria (fig. 72). An interesting series of styles was started at a ful bili in 1960, when girls plaited their hair in parallel rows. This was later plastered with a black oil mixture (fig. 73) (on another occasion it was a bright blue mixture). In 1974, at yet another ful bili, that style had evolved to plaited rows that converged at the crown of the head (fig. 74); and finally in 1981, I saw a woman with the rows converging into a top knot (fig. 75).

While the participation of young women in the ful bili was the most striking and dramatic instance of the deliberate elaboration of hairstyle, at virtually all public festivals—indeed at all occasions—young women took particular care in their hair. It was not uncommon to see groups of women and girls sitting under a tree doing each other's hair. This was a social activity with all of the collateral benefits of an association of young peers. They gossiped, they joked, and above all they learned, as they were socialized into adolescence and into womanhood.

I must admit that during that first field research, my sensitivity to feminine styles was heightened because I had my five-year-old daughter with me. She, of course, was learning her early feminine identification, and as a result she was partic-

Fig. 74. Girls in a crowd showing both the older style of parallel hair rows (third from left) and the then new style of radial rows.
Photo: James H. Vaughan, 1974.

Fig. 75. A style of radial rows culminating
in a top knot.
Photo: James H. Vaughan, 1981.

ularly perceptive of the way women behaved. She tried to emulate Margi women, from the way they dressed to the way they walked; she even complained that her blond hair was unlike theirs. I owe much of my knowledge of the behavior of Margi women to the observations and comments of that small child. (The infant in fig. 71 is named "Susie" after my daughter.)

Today Margi raiment has evolved. After the late 1960s, bare-breasted women in traditional clothing were rarely seen. The influences of Islam, Christianity, and modern Nigerian fashion have radically altered clothing. Most of the ritual life has changed, and contemporary ful bilis are anemic versions of the earlier festivals. Most women cover their heads in public, though in private places one may see an elaborate hairstyle that would otherwise go unseen (fig. 76), and one still sees young women resting in the heat of the day and arranging hair. Clearly, within the new constraints, they nonetheless take great pride in their personal appearance, including their hair.

I wish to conclude with a caution: it is easy to fall into the trap of thinking of these more traditional Africans as wearing "costumes" and prescribed "tribal" hairstyles, "tribal" markings, etc. In my opinion, this view—"the unchanging primitive,

Fig. 76. A young woman with an elaborate hairstyle, taken in the privacy of her home compound. Outside she wore a head covering.
Photo: James H. Vaughan, 1987.

ever the captive of custom"—is not only inaccurate but fails to appreciate the full range of creativity that is characteristic of all societies. Hairstyle, like culture, evolves with time and circumstance. Moreover, hairstyle, probably more than most customs, is subject to deliberate change and individual creativity. It is precisely because hairstyles reflect creativity that I believe they are an appropriate subject for an art museum. To speak of "traditional costume" or "traditional hairstyle" may ignore cultural dynamics and human creativity, and in fact is often a statement of the observers' limited purview more than a picture of a culture. In summary, although clothing, hairstyles, and other markers may be important as differentiations of ethnicity, gender, or class, they are not immune to change. Furthermore, in my experience among the Margi nothing was quite so changeable as hairstyles; indeed I found young Margi women much like American youths in their interest in new fashions.

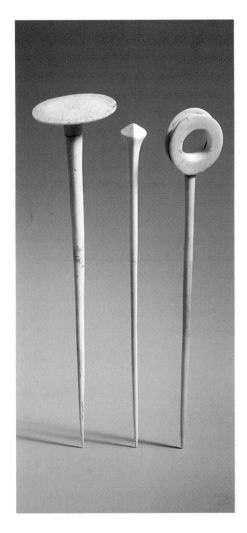

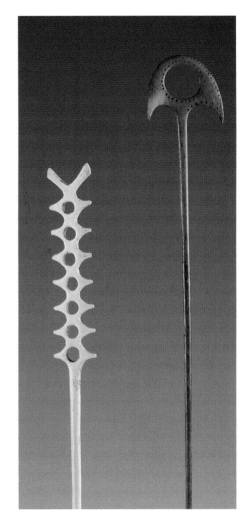

Cat. III a+b
Hairpins
Mangbetu or Zande, Democratic Republic
of Congo
Ivory. H: 25.5 and 23.5 cm.
Marc and Denyse Ginzberg Collection

Cat. III c
Hairpin
Zande, Democratic Republic of Congo
Ivory. H: 24.4 cm.
Marc and Denyse Ginzberg Collection

Cat. III d
Two hairpins
Mangbetu, Democratic Republic of Congo
Ivory. H: 14.6 cm. (both)
Marc and Denyse Ginzberg Collection

Cat. III e
Hairpin
Mangbetu or Zande, Democratic Republic
of Congo
Ivory. H: 27.4 cm.
Etnografisch Museum, Antwerp; Gift F.M. Olbrechts

Cat. III f
Hairpin
Mangbetu or Zande, Democratic Republic
of Congo
Ivory. H: 32 cm.
Etnografisch Museum, Antwerp;
Gift Handelsmuseum (1916)

Mangbetu Hairstyles and the Art of Seduction: *Lipombo*

Els DE PALMENAER

This essay focuses on the hairstyles and skull-elongation practices of the Mangbetu, and to a lesser extent on some of the coiffures of their neighbors the Zande, both of them from the Uele and Bomokandi river basin in northeastern Congo. This region, a transition area between the savanna in the country's north and the equatorial forest in the south, is inhabited by a number of ethnic groups of historically diverse origins. The Mangbetu are closely related culturally and belong to the Eastern Central Sudanese language group. Their most important neighbors, the Zande, speak a Ubangi language (Burssens 1992:11). Despite their linguistic and political differences, however, the material culture of these groups cannot be discussed separately, and they share common views on body ornamentation.

In the past, the people of this area devoted a great deal of attention to body art. The upper classes of the Mangbetu, for example, painted their bodies in geometric patterns for dances and other festivities, using the juice of the gardenia plant. Both sexes also applied scarification (mainly on the chest and back, rarely on the face), while the women pierced their earlobes with little wooden, iron, or ivory rods (Burssens 1992:20). Wealthy individuals could spare the time to have their hair fixed in elaborate styles. They further embellished their hair with combs and hairpins or a straw hat. The Mangbetu and groups under their influence also paid special attention to the shape of their heads, practicing a custom of extreme skull elongation that remained in vogue until about the middle of this century (Schildkrout and Keim 1990:126–27).

Body ornamentation and a variety of hairstyles, which represented the status of the wearer or were intended for particular occasions, changed considerably over the course of the nineteenth century and especially during the twentieth. Enid Schildkrout and Curtis Keim, in *African Reflections*, their recent book on the peoples of the northeastern Congo, note that "change is most evident in the material culture of northeastern Zaïre [Congo] in reference to the repertoire of objects that adorn the human body. . . . Because body art is transportable and ephemeral, as is the body itself, it tends to follow fads and fashions more than any other art form, in northeast-

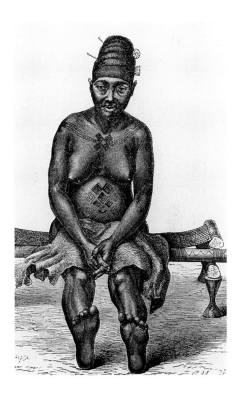

Fig. 77. "Première femme de Bongua." First wife of Chief Bongua with a basket coiffure adorned with hairpins and combs. Uele region, Democratic Republic of Congo.
Drawing by O. Mathieu 19th century

Fig. 78. "Bunsa, ein Sohn Munsa's."
Bunsa, son of the Mangbetu king Mbunza
is wearing a woven hat, attached to his
coiffure with long hatpins.
Drawing by George Schweinfurth, 1870.

ern Zaïre as elsewhere" (1990:123). Hairstyles that were highly fashionable around the turn of the century, for example, and were at first the exclusive privilege of the ruling Mangbetu classes, evolved into a common ideal of beauty among several ethnic groups of the northeastern Congo.

The anthropomorphic sculpture of the region provides an important source of information on hairstyles and body ornamentation. Body embellishments are meticulously represented in statues and figurative objects such as terra-cotta pottery, weapons, musical instruments, bark boxes, and pipe bowls. It is also possible to sketch a representative picture of earlier hairstyles in the region on the basis of nineteenth-century travel literature and illustrations.

Explorations of the northeastern Congo by Europeans commenced in the middle of the nineteenth century, when naturalists, traders, adventurers, and colonizers crossed the vast region. One ambition of these explorers was to map the ethnic groups they encountered, and they were interested in the sophisticated coiffures of the Mangbetu, making their reports a valuable source of data on local hairstyles of the period.

One of the first Westerners to visit the Mangbetu was the German botanist G. Schweinfurth, who spent some weeks at the court of the Mangbetu king Mbunza in 1870. Enthralled with the culture of the region, Schweinfurth described the king's power and splendor in lyrical terms. His much-read travelogue *Im Herzen von Afrika* (The heart of Africa, 1874) gave the Mangbetu widespread fame and for decades shaped the views of later explorers and colonizers (Burssens 1992:7). Schweinfurth made copious notes on some of the hairstyles in vogue at the time. He also illustrated some of these. A typical coiffure worn by both men and women of the Mangbetu upper classes, as well as by those of the Zande.

In the second half of the nineteenth century, the basket hairstyle was a status symbol. The hair was braided at the crown of the head into a kind of backward tilted chignon, supported by a reed frame. Delicate braids created a broad band around the forehead. Because the hair at the temples was too short to be connected with the chignon, "foreign" hair had to be added, which was obtained from the deceased or from victims of war (Schweinfurth 1875, I:491; II:53). The portrait "First Wife of chief Bongua" (fig. 77) shows the basket hairstyle, which in this case includes a wooden comb and hairpins.[1]

In the portrait "Bunsa a Son of Munsa," the son of the Mangbetu king Mbunza wears a small hat on top of his basket coiffure (fig. 78). From the late nineteenth century to the beginning of the twentieth, reed hats, cylindrical at the bottom and usually rectangular at the top, were the privilege of men. They were fastened to the tips of the coiffure with large hat pins (cat. 111). As a rule, women embellished their hair only with hairpins, but later they too occasionally wore hats at dances (Schildkrout and Keim 1990:123, 133). Schweinfurth also paid attention to the unusual blond locks of Prince Bunsa (1875, II:52). He observed blond hair in about one fifth of Mbunza's subjects, and concluded that the Mangbetu were in this respect very different from their neighbors the Zande (ibid.:92). Schweinfurth's account of this exceptional phenomenon fascinated later anthropologists and colonizers. Although he suggested the possibility of a kind of albinoism in Prince Bunsa, a real explanation was never given, and the phenomenon was never unambiguously confirmed by other travelers.

Around the turn of the century, Waquez and De Renette declared that they had not seen the putative blond hair, but they did notice that the hair of Mangbetu women appeared more chestnut brown than black (Van Overbergh and De Jonghe 1909:117). The Dominican priest M. H. Lelong even suggested that the Mangbetu bleached their hair when Schweinfurth encountered them in 1870 (1946, I:76).

Several explorers during the early 1880s described the typical basket hairstyle illustrated in Schweinfurth's travelogue. Gaetano Casati, for example, noted that "their hair is the object of the most meticulous care; it is combed, curled, and arranged in a thousand different ways, always to arrive at a kind of backward tilted cylinder" (1892:84).[2] Wilhelm Junker described how these artfully created hairstyles held their shape for weeks (1882–86:306). Unlike Schweinfurth and Casati, Junker also observed how the Mangbetu elongated the heads of babies by binding them with a band of raffia fibers.

Information on hairstyles after the beginning of the twentieth century is more plentiful and verifiable, since scientists, colonizers, and missionaries took photographs on the spot. In 1908, a change took place that would be crucial to the fate of the northeastern peoples: the Uele territory, which, since 1891, had been part of the Congo Free State (the personal possession of the Belgian King Leopold II), was transferred to the Belgian state. The Belgian government recruited colonial officers to collect "knowledge" of the local population that might be of service to the administration. Between 1911 and 1913, an ethnographic expedition was sent to the Uele and Ubangi territories, under the command of A. Hutereau, a Belgian lieutenant who had previously done research in the region (Schildkrout and Keim 1990:41). Hutereau's photographs (fig. 79) and the countless objects he collected ended up at the Musée royal du Congo belge (now the Royal Museum for Central Africa, Tervuren). An expedition under the auspices of the American Museum of Natural History (1909–15), led by the zoologists H. Lang and J. Chapin, also resulted in vast collections, relevant publications, and photographs of the people of the northeastern Congo.

These photographs and publications show that new hairstyles had been developed around the turn of the century, and that the basket coiffure had gone out of fashion. The custom of elongating the head had originally been the privilege of the ruling Mangbetu classes; by the early twentieth century, it had become more common among the Mangbetu, and was also copied by some of the neighboring groups. To make the skull seem even more elongated, Mangbetu women wore a kind of funnel-shaped coiffure. This style, originally symbolic of high social status, was considered exceptionally attractive, and took a lot of

Fig. 79. "Wife of Chief Bambili."
Sande, Bambili, Uele region Democratic Republic of Congo.
Photo: A. Hutereau, 1912.

Fig. 80. Mangbetu women's attire, Uele region Democratic Republic of Congo.
Photographer: Zagourski, 1926-1937.

time to create (figs. 80, 81). The funnel shape was made by pulling back the strands of hair, if necessary supplementing them with "foreign" hair, and tying them into a bun that was open at the back and worked into the hair by means of a disc-shaped frame of woven reed. To make the coiffure even more elegant, the forehead was wrapped with a broad band of carefully arranged pieces of black string, and finally everything was decorated with hairpins and combs (Burssens 1992:18).

Women of lower status wore their hair more simply, as did women of high status when they were not at public functions. Lang noted during the expedition of 1909–15 that "the Mangbetu women very often change their style of hairdressing according to their moods. The basketlike type, however, if once adopted is seldom abandoned. It needs rather long hair and women are proud of it" (quoted in Schildkrout and Keim 1990:127). The Belgian commander Laplume, who worked in the Uele region from 1893 to 1911, saw women spending two hours and more to fix their hair in different styles. The hair was first rubbed with palm oil to make it shine, then separated with a comb or a small iron rod, before being braided. Men preferred to wear their hair short, sometimes shaved in striking patterns or even completely bald. During periods of mourning, women "broke" their coiffure (fig. 82), or, in exceptional cases, had their heads completely shaved as a sign of mourning for a deceased husband (Van Overbergh and De Jonghe 1909:132, 357).

Fig. 81. Preferred wife of Kongolis with characteristic basketlike coiffure crowned with halo.
Makere (Mangbetu), Uele region, Democratic Republic of Congo.
Photo: Herbert Lang expedition, 1909-1915.

Photographs by Lang and Hutereau (figs. 79 and 83) show hairstyles in vogue among the ruling class of the Avongura/Zande. Hutereau pointed out certain differences between the southern Zande groups from the Bomokandi region and the Zande from the area north of the Uele river: only the southern Zande, for example, adopted the Mangbetu skull shape, and some of the Mangbetu hairstyles were also fashionable with them (Hutereau 1921:229). The wives of Zande rulers south of the Bomokandi wore their hair in a style that, like the Mangbetu coiffures, involved braiding their own hair along with "foreign" strands in the shape of a disc (fig. 79). This coiffure, called *bagbadi*, was in fact a fan-shaped wig, but was rarely taken off. The disc was attached to the hair with a few loose knots (Lang Archives, AMNH 2565, Hutereau D. E. 312). In contrast to the rather more funnel-shaped Mangbetu style, which ended in an outward halo, the heads of Zande women were encircled with a garland of radiating braids, and the entire creation was further adorned with cowries or teeth, often from dogs (Czekanowski 1924:33, 1927:19–21).

Of the ornaments that embellished the hairstyles of the Zande, Mangbetu, and related ethnic groups, combs were reserved for women. According to Jan Czekanowski (1924:33), the hat pins and hairpins of the Mangbetu and Zande are indistinguishable. The pins were worn by both sexes and were made of bone, ivory, or metal (brass, iron, and copper) (cat. 111). There are also rare wooden examples. The simple pieces consist of a thin rod crowned with a spearhead, a disc, a star, a trident,

Fig. 82. "Coiffures des femmes."
Mangbetu, Uele region Democratic
Republic of Congo. The "broken" coif-
fures are possibly a sign of mourning.
Photo: R.F. Marcolin, 1945.

Fig. 83. Nasara,
one of the wives of Akenge with typical
fan-shaped style of the Zande, Democratic
Republic of Congo.
Photo: Herbert Lang expedition, 1909-1915.

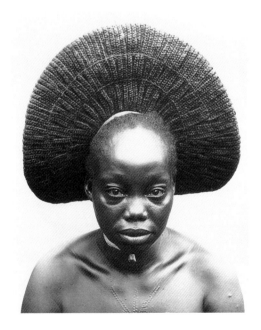

or a sickle-shaped design. The more intricate pins are also worked in the middle. The most valuable hat pins and hairpins were made of ivory and were considered status symbols. Making them required a steady hand and great skill: the massive tip of an elephant's tooth was used to carve the disc-shaped crown. According to Lang, the discs of the long ivory pins represented the radiance of the sun, and were symbolic of wealth and high social status (Schildkrout and Keim 1990:131).

Men usually wore pins to attach a straw hat to their hair, while women wore them in the hair itself. In addition, notes by both Lang and Hutereau show that hat pins and hairpins were used for several different purposes at the beginning of the twentieth century: they could be used to clean small wounds, to remove chiggers, to care for fingernails and toenails, or as a kind of knife to trim one's hair. They also fulfilled an important role as gifts exchanged between lovers (Lang, in Schildkrout and Keim 1990:133–34; Hutereau 1911:D. E. 312, Tervuren).

Westerners found the elaborate hairstyles, scarification, and especially the anatomical deformation of the heads of the Mangbetu "bizarre" yet also "attractive." In colonial propaganda, the characteristic Mangbetu profile fit the stereotype of the ideal African man or woman. Mangbetu women with a halo-shaped coiffure adorned with pins, and Mangbetu men in a broad forehead-band and straw hat, appeared on propagandistic postcards and on a series of stamps under the title "indigenous peo-ple, animals, and landscapes" (fig. 85). In addition, realistic ebony statuettes and especially female Mangbetu busts were made in different places and sold in large numbers; they can still be found in many a Belgian household (Burssens 1992:7).

When and how the Mangbetu decided to elongate their skulls is not clear. According to oral traditions, the custom was introduced by the Mangbetu kings (Schildkrout and Keim 1990:125). The habit of treating infants to make them dolicho-cephalic by massaging or winding cords around their skulls was also found among other African peoples in earlier times. Although deliberate skull deformation is not unique to the Mangbetu, they are the African people most renowned for it.

Elongation started with newborns when the skull had not yet grown hard. From the first day after the baby was born, the Mangbetu started to wrap a band of raffia fibers or human hair around its skull. The baby's head was oiled and the band was regularly loosened. The step-by-step deformation took about eight to nine months, until the skull had taken the right shape (Schildkrout and Keim 1990:124–25, Reisgids Belgisch Congo 1958:330). The process pulled the skin back tightly and slanted the eyelids upward, which was also considered very attractive. The making of these bands was labor-intensive women's work. The fibers were first blackened, then rubbed with mud, and finally cleaned carefully and wound around a spool.

Skull elongation, which was a status symbol among the Mangbetu ruling classes at the beginning of the century and was later emulated by neighboring groups, evolved into a common ideal of beauty among the peoples of the northeastern Congo. According to Schildkrout and Keim, the tradition survived until the middle of this century, when it was outlawed by the Belgian government (1990:262).[3] Although the heads of children are no longer bound, older people in the region still have elongated skulls.

A photograph by H. Goldstein (fig. 84) and comments by the Belgian priest Lelong (1946:70–90) show that some of the Mangbetu continued to practice skull elongation until at least the end of the 1940s. They still considered a long skull extremely appealing, and used the Bangala/Lingala word *lipombo*

bo for the custom. According to Lelong, the word "lipombo" summarizes all of the Mangbetu's views on body art and social mores. It corresponds roughly to our notions of "coquetry, elegance, and display," or can be translated simply as "chic." Although some mothers even then no longer practiced the custom with their children, their opinions about it were clear: "A Mangbetu with a flat head is a diminished being."[4] The funnel-shaped hairstyle, with braided hair supported by a reed frame, was only used as part of the ceremonial dress of wealthy women and was gradually going out of fashion. Part of the reason was that it was hard to carry loads on such fragile hair. Furthermore it had to be protected when sleeping by the use of a headrest. Another factor was the growing indifference toward traditional customs. As a result, new hairstyles were created, easier to wear but just as carefully arranged. Since the 1940s, both classical styles and unusually clever and extravagant combinations have been used. The Mangbetu have always considered hairstyles that show a rich imagination to be the most appealing, and that trend continues to this day.

Fig. 84. "Mother and child." Makere (Mangbetu), Uele region Democratic Republic of Congo. Photographer: H. Goldstein, Congopresse, 1949.

Fig. 85. Stamps showing a Mangbetu man and woman. Printed as colonial propaganda for the Belgian Colony as part of a series entitled "indigenous people, animals and landscapes." Print: Graphic Institute of Paris. Engraving: Stamp Printers Mechelen, 1931.
Stefan Henau Collection, Belgium.

1. G. Schweinfurth notes what a privilege it was for him to get permission from Bongua to make a portrait of the chief's wife. In return for her patience while she sat for the portrait, Schweinfurth allowed her to run her fingers through his hair, which he thought was tantamount to "la plus grande faveur que je pusse accorder aux indigènes" (the greatest favor I could bestow on the natives) (1875: 490–91).

2. "La coiffure est l'objet des soins les plus attentifs, les cheveux sont peigné, frisés, arrangés de mille façons pour arriver toujours à une sorte de cylindre incliné en arrière."

3. Schildkrout and Keim do not elaborate on the prohibition (1990:262, endnote 23). Additional research in the "Wetboek van Strafrecht van de Kolonie"—the Colonial Penal Code (1940–59)—did not turn up anything. It is possible that skull elongation was designated as "voluntary bodily harm" or "barbaric practice," which would have made it punishable by law. On the other hand, it is also possible that the prohibition was included in other sources of law, such as police regulations decreed by a colonial governing body (N. Vanderscheuren, personal communication, University of Gent, 1999).

4. "Un Mangbetu à tête plat est un être diminué."

Tools and Ornaments

The tools of the hairdresser include pins, combs, and razors. Scissors did not appear south of the Sahara until introduced by North African leather workers and by European missionaries and colonials.

The coiffeurs often included extensions of hair or fibers, clay, coloring ingredients, ornaments of gold and other metals, coral, glass beads (usually imported), stone beads (often indigenous), ostrich-eggshell beads (always locally produced), fruit seeds, shells, and leather. Indeed the list seems endless.

Loyer reports of the inhabitants of Issini on the Ivory Coast that *"of their Hair they are mighty careful . . . , tying it up in an hundred different Fashions. They comb it with a wooden or Ivory Fork, with four Teeth, which is always fastened on their Head. They also anoint their Hair with Palm-Oil and Charcoal, as they do their Bodies, to keep it black and make it grow. They adorn it with small Toys of Gold, or pretty Shells, each striving to outvie an other in their Finery. THEY shave themselves with Knives, which they temper so, as to fall little short of Razors. Some only shave one half of the Head, dressing the other like a Night-Cap cocked over one Ear. Others leave broad Patches here and there unshaved in different Forms, according to their Fancy. They are fond of their Beards and comb them daily wearing them as long as the Turks"* (Astley II:435). [R.S.]

OPPOSITE
Fig. 86. Fulani woman, French Guinea.
Photo: F.R. Roberts, early 20th century.

Cat. 112
Hair ornament
Fulani, West Africa
Wood. H: 6.4 cm.
Drs. Jean and Noble Endicott

Cat. 113
Razors
Kuba, Democratic Republic of Congo
Metal. H: 16.3 - 19.5 cm.
Roy and Sophia Sieber
Mona Gavigan/Affrica

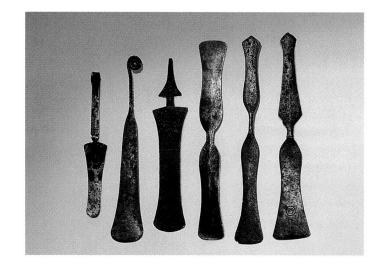

Cat. 114
Comb
Bamana, Mali
Wood. H: 29.7 cm.
Etnografisch Museum, Antwerp;
Gift Olbrechts (1975)

Cat. 115
Comb
Baule, Côte d'Ivoire
Wood, gold, thread. H: 15.6 cm.
National Museum of African Art,
Gift of Judith Timyan

Cat. 116
Comb
Baule, Côte d'Ivoire
Wood, gold, thread. H: 10.1 cm.
National Museum of African Art,
Gift of Judith Timyan

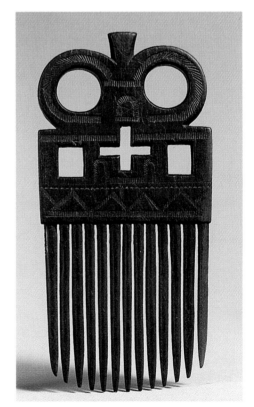

Cat. 117
Comb
Ashanti, Ghana
Wood. H: 27.3 cm.
Private Collection

Cat. 118
Comb
Ashanti, Ghana
Wood. H: 30 cm.
Joyce Marie Sims

Cat. 119
Comb
Ashanti, Ghana
Wood, pigment. H: 33.5 cm.
Amyas Naegele

Cat. 120
Comb
Lugura or Kaguru, Tanzania
Wood. H: 15.5 cm.
Joyce Marie Sims

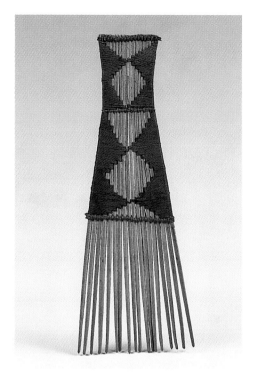

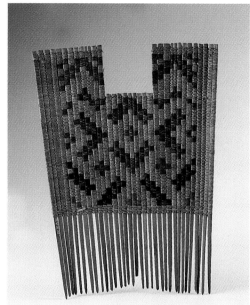

ABOVE LEFT
Cat. 123
Comb
Kuba (?), Democratic Republic of Congo
Wood, fibers. H: 24.1 cm.
Etnografisch Museum, Antwerp;
Gift Olbrechts (1975)

ABOVE RIGHT
Cat. 124
Comb
Kenya (?)
Metal. H: 9.5 cm.
Roy and Sophia Sieber

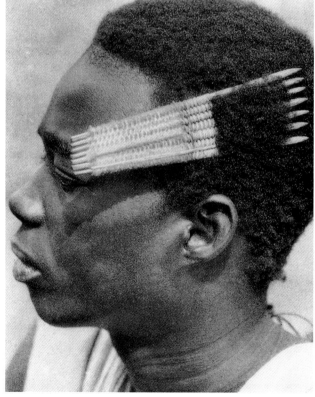

TOP
Cat. 121
Comb
Democratic Republic of Congo (?)
Reed, copper, brass wire. H: 23.9 cm.
Etnografisch Museum, Antwerp; Gift F.M. Olbrechts
(1975)

BOTTOM
Cat. 122
Comb
East Africa
Wood. H: 13 cm.
Private Collection

Fig. 87. Man with comb as hair ornament,
Kassanga, Guinea.
Photo: Bernatzik, early 20th century.

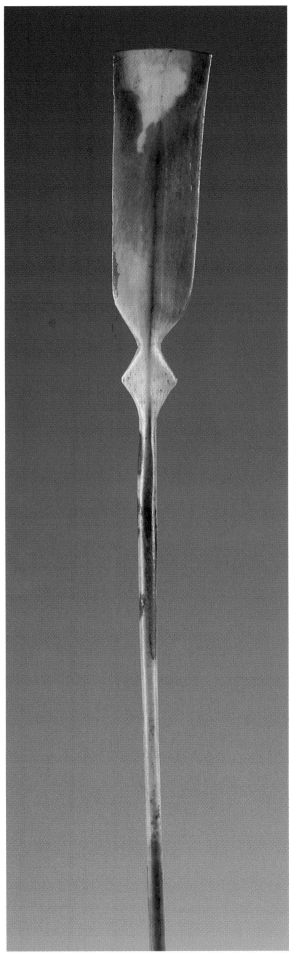

Cat. 125
Hairpin
Dogon(?), Mali
Bronze. H: 23.2 cm.
The Graham Collection

Cat. 126
Hairpin
East Africa (?) or Zulu, South Africa
Ivory. H: 34.3 cm.
Etnografisch Museum, Antwerp;
Gift Handelsmuseum (1916)

Cat. 127
Four Combs
Kaniok, Yaka or Suku,
Democratic Republic of Congo
Wood. H: 15-23 cm.
Etnografisch Museum, Antwerp;
(a) Purchased from Pareyn (1920),
(b-d) Gift F.M. Olbrechts (1975)

Cat. 128
Comb
Yaka, Democratic Republic of Congo
Wood. H: 17 cm.
Private Collection

Fig. 88. Men at the annual celebration
in Tiker quarter,
Warwar, Mambila, Cameroon.
*Photo: Gil Schneider, 1948, courtesy of Evan
Schneider.*

Fig. 89. Men's hairdressing,
Sango, Upper Mobangi River,
Democratic Republic of Congo.
*Photo: The Minister of Colonies, Belgium,
early 20th century.*

OPPOSITE
Cat. 129
Crest mask
Zombo, Angola and Democratic
Republic of Congo
Wood, fibers, beads, buttons. H: 19 cm.
Felix Collection

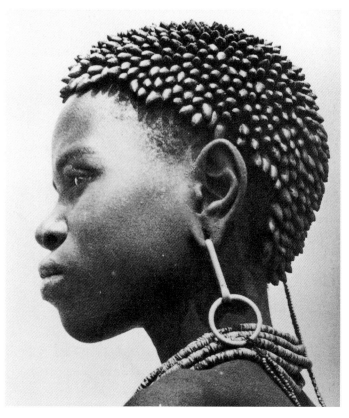

ABOVE, LEFT TO RIGHT

Fig. 90. Bride with ostrich eggshells and copper beads, as well as fruit pips in their hair. !Xu, Bushman (San), Namibia.
Photo: Dr. Ernst R. Scherz, 1940s.

Fig. 91. Witch doctor with beads and cowrie-shells attached to his hair, Kxoé, Bushman (San), Namibia.
Photo: Anneliese Scherz, 1940s.

Fig. 92. Married woman, Nyaneka, Angola.
Photo: Anneliese Scherz, 1940s.

Fig. 93. *Omelenda* hairstyle made of sinew and fruit pips, Kwaluudhi and Ngandjera, Wambo group, Namibia.
Photo: Anneliese Scherz, 1940s.

Fig. 94. Woman with wig and hair ornaments, southwest Angola.
Photo: Centro de Informação e Turismo de Angola, Gabinete Fotográfico.

Congo Français
201. - Vieille femme pahouine

Fig. 95. Old woman, Fang, Gabon.
Photo: J. Audema, ca. 1905.

Fig. 96. Woman with feather and other hair ornaments, Oulad-Hamid, Sudan.
Photo: Bernatzik, first half of 20th century.

Fig. 97. A Turkana man, Kenya.
Photo: Cudahy-Massee-Milwaukee Museum African Expedition, 1928-29.

Fig. 98. Nziri man, Central African Republic.
Photo: J. Audema, ca. 1905.

Cat. 130
Hair Ornament
Zemba, Southern Angola
Lather, fiber, bullet casings, tin. H: 29 cm.
Amyas Naegele

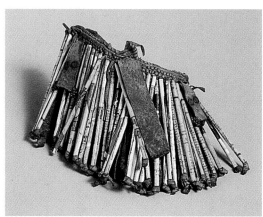

CONGO FRANÇAIS et dépen
Type Banziri - Bas-Kouang

Collection J. Audema

Hair Matters in
South Central Africa

Manuel JORDÁN

Fig. 99. V. L. Cameron (1877) published this illustration showing "hair-dressing" in Angola. The elaborate coiffure frames the wearer's face and supports two hair buns that protrude from the top. The elaborate hairstyle reflects the high social status of its wearer.

Hair and Ethnicity

Related and neighboring peoples of Angola, the Democratic Republic of the Congo, and Zambia have customarily dressed and embellished their hair, treating the head to sumptuous hairstyles defined as sculptural forms through a combination of braids, tresses, buns, lobes, and wings.[1] Well-kept hairstyles reflect beauty, health, well-being, and often social status or rank (fig. 99). Unkempt hair (*isasa dansuki* in the southern Lunda language) is seen as inappropriate and a poor reflection on an individual.[2] Because a haircut or hairdo commonly requires the assistance of a friend or relative, individuals who continuously keep their hair in disarray may be regarded as socially peripheral, having no one willing to assist or care for them.[3]

Hair serves as a form of individual expression, but specific hairdos or coiffures reflect regional hairstyles, and some, favored by particular groups, are associated with their own sense of ethnic identity.[4] Chokwe people of Angola, the Democratic Republic of the Congo, and Zambia configure their *tota* hairstyle by making very short braids that they carefully knot to form numerous pellets that are covered with red clay and oil. *Lenge* is another popular hairstyle, defined by longer braids that are woven and tied to create horizontal bands, packed closely together and similarly maintained with red clay and oil. *Chisukusuku* strings of thinly braided hair may be incorporated into both styles as a looser element on the tightly packed coiffures (Bastin 1961:144). Variations of these hairstyles, commonly worn by men and women through the 1960s, were reproduced as wigs (*uyembe*) made from hair and/or vegetal fibers (fig. 100). The *tota* and *lenge* hairstyles, along with scarification marks such as the forehead *chingelyengelye* cross motif, are traits that have distinguished the Chokwe from their various neighbors for over a century.[5]

The Ovimbundu, Chokwe neighbors to the west in central Angola, dress their hair in different ways, but their most distinctive style includes long loops that hang low toward the back. Wilfrid Hambly (1934:131) provides an excellent description of this hairstyle: "Ovimbundu women braid their hair neatly in strands across their fore-

Fig. 100. This wig or *uyembe*, made from fibers, imitates the *tota* hairstyle favored by the Chokwe. Oil and red powder would have been applied to its surface to maintain the piece and give it a more "natural" look. Collection of the Birmingham Museum of Art, 1997.136.

OPPOSITE
Cat. 131
Face mask
Ngangela, Angola
Wood, fiber. H: 27 cm.
Private Collection, Belgium

heads, and small blue and white beads are used to decorate the braids. The hair-dressing of the Ovimbundu women is different from that in any other part of Angola. At an early age, the hair is trained into two long loops at the back of the head. Then these are covered with black cloth which is bound tightly. The two loops are afterwards studded with brass-headed tacks obtained from a store."

In south-central Angola, the Ngangela cluster of related peoples[6] commonly wear a tight hairdo characterized by conical arched lobes toward the back of the head, but shoulder-length strings of braided hair are also favored (cat. 131). The looser hairstyle is also worn by women in southwestern Angola. An elaborate version of this hairstyle, covered with beads, shells, and imported buttons, is typical of Mwila women. The hairstyle, called *omphoha*, is represented in Mwila dolls that are used in the context of female initiation (cat. 132, fig. 101). The dolls are made by the initiates and kept until they give birth to their first child. Related peoples in the region use a similar hairstyle for their female initiates, who allow the numerous braids to cover their faces during their puberty rituals (Estermann 1983, II:96a).

The Mwila, as well as their Humbe, Ngambwe, Ndimba, Herrero, and Kwanyama neighbors of southwestern Angola and northern Namibia,[7] create a number of highly elaborate coiffures that combine arched cascading bands of hair toward the back of the head, thick strands of mud-packed hair, and large wings on the sides of the head. The coiffures are heavily decorated with imported beads and other decorative items.

Although imported wigs and new hairstyles are present among these groups, the predominant hairstyles in some areas of Angola have been in fashion for over a hundred years. The published accounts of European officers, explorers, ethnographers, and missionaries who traveled through the interior of Central Africa in the nineteenth century offer numerous illustrations that correlate distinctive hairstyles with specific ethnic groups.[8] Many of these hairstyles still prevail and help, at least superficially, to suggest an individual's ethnic identity.

Exclusive Hairstyles

Along with status symbols such as beaded crowns, headdresses, and diadems, specific hairstyles were meant to be worn exclusively by chiefs or high-ranking dignitaries. One relatively common hairstyle associated with Central African chiefs takes the form of a horned coiffure, where the "horns," created with braided or bundled hair that may be covered with cloth, protrudes from the sides and/or top of the head in a straight or slightly curved fashion.[9] H. A. Dias de Carvalho (1890:401) illustrated an "audience" in which a Lunda paramount, called Mucanza, is easily distinguished by his coiffure (fig. 102). The chief figures prominently at the center, seated on a stool that is placed on a straw mat, but it is his horned coiffure that most clearly differentiates him from the others. The other men, probably his warriors, wear less formal coiffures, including versions of the tota and chisukusuku hairstyles. The illustration shows a correlation between hairstyles and social stature: whereas the chief wears an exclusive coiffure, the warriors have hairstyles that are indicative of their class (or adulthood), and the boys, probably assistants, show the simpler hair.

Certain haircuts may similarly indicate social class or status. An early-twentieth-century postcard from the Belgian Congo (today's Democratic Republic of the

Fig. 101. Girl with her doll, Mwila,
Angola.
Photo: Afrika Museum, Berg en Dal.

Cat. 132
Fertility figure/doll
Mwila, Angola
Wood, fiber, beads. H: 22.5 cm.
National Museum of Ethnology, Lisbon

Fig. 102. Carvalho (1890) published this illustration of a Lunda chief wearing a horned coiffure. The chief's warriors wear less elaborate hairstyles while the "attendants" show simple hair.

Fig. 103. Some types of royal crown may have evolved from elaborate hairstyles. This 1932 gouache portrait (signed "Renault") shows Lunda chief Mwene Mbishi with a crown that may derive from one of the "cascading" hairstyles that are common in central Africa. *Private collection.*

Fig. 104. This early twentieth century postcard, from the "Belgian Congo" (now the Democratic Republic of the Congo), shows "Bangala" (or Imbangala) men with heavily scarified faces and choices of haircut (one with a shaved head) that may indicate their social status. Undated, unknown photographer. *Private collection.*

Congo) (fig. 104) depicts four Imbangala men standing in line. Three of the men show short haircuts with "hairlines" shaved in a stylized fashion. Their scarified faces certainly indicate that these are adult, fully initiated men, and the choices of haircut (one fully shaved at the front) may relate to class, clan, or ethnic hierarchies.

Some crowns and headdresses worn by Central African chiefs and dignitaries (Capello and Ivens 1881, Cardoso 1903) find their prototype in royal European crowns or military helmets. Other crowns may actually be the result of an elaboration of hairstyles that were first replicated as wigs and later constructed and adorned as royal headdresses. The headdresses may be constructed from cloth and fibers to which feathers and decorative beaded patterns are added to reflect the status of the wearer. These simpler crowns/headdresses allowed chiefs to have simple haircuts on which the crowns were attached in a manner similar to a wig. A 1932 painted portrait (signed "Renault") of Lunda Chief Mwene Mbishi, from Dilolo, Democratic Republic of the Congo, shows the royal character wearing a beaded crown that may very well find its prototype in one of the "cascading" hairstyles that are common in Central Africa (fig 103).

Hair Implements

To create, maintain, support, and adorn the hair a variety of implements are manufactured and utilized. Different types of hairpins, combs, and brushes are still commonly made in Central Africa (cats. 133-135). These implements are sometimes combined so that there is a comb on one end and a brush on the other. Combs, hair picks, and pins are used in building and maintaining coiffures, but also serve as decorative items when inserted and worn on the hair.[10] The quality of the manufactured item and the material of choice reflect the wealth and status of the wearer. A carved figurative wooden comb with abstract decorative patterns is more valuable than a nonfigurative comb, or a comb made from cane or wires. An elaborately carved ivory comb or hairpin requires even more work and the material makes it less common/affordable.[11] Fine hair-implements are considered a luxury and many become treasured items that are inherited through generations. As

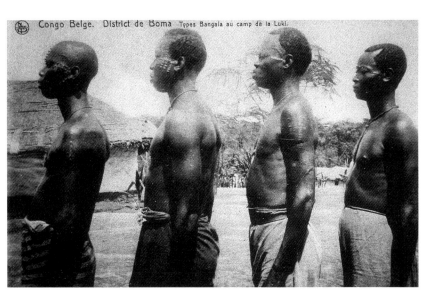

Congo Belge. District de Boma Types Bangala au camp de la Luki.

in the case of other sculptural forms and utilitarian objects, Chokwe and neighboring peoples may actually keep or wear an inherited piece to honor the memory and spirit of the original owner.

A great variety of found, imported, or manufactured items are used to decorate coiffures. Beads, shells, metal tacks, and strips of cloth may be used to add color and texture to different hairstyles. Short and hollow wooden sticks, seeds, and plastic or metal bottle-caps may also be added to braids, to rattle or sound when the head is moved around during ritual/ceremonial dances. In such occasions the hair becomes an active element of performance, whereas visually and audibly it brings an additional dimension to dances that generally mark individual or social transitions.[12]

The Matter of Hair

As matter or substance, hair is understood to have certain qualities that relate to the "life" or potency of its owner.[13] This may be because hair (like toe- and fingernails) grows in an accelerated fashion compared to the rest of the human body. It may also be because after death, the hair may appear to grow a little, while other parts of the body are in a state of decay.[14] One concern of some people is that their hair be handled by someone who is trusted. That is because, in the wrong hands, hair may be used as a powerful substance to afflict its owner. A victim's hair is often included in charms or "medicines" of witchcraft.[15] Witches are also said to rob graves to collect human parts, including hair and nails, to activate evil supernatural creatures to act on their behalf.[16] In this context the "power" of hair is equated with the power of (a) life. A less sinister but related practice is to use someone's hair in "love" medicines.

Cat. 133
Comb
Chokwe, Angola/Democratic Republic of Congo
Wood. H: 15.7 cm.
Corice and Armand P. Arman

Cat. 134
Comb
Lwimbi, Angola
Wood, metal. H: 15.9 cm.
Drs. Jean and Noble Endicott

Cat. 135
Comb
Chokwe, Angola
Wood. H: 15 cm.
Joyce Marie Sims

If a person's hair is acquired and added to charms or other substances, the will of the victim succumbs to the erotic aspirations of the pursuer.[17]

Besides hair, all the decorative items applied to a coiffure (beads, seeds, etc.) may be similarly used against the wearer if they happen to fall off and are not immediately retrieved by the owner or a friend. This is most typically seen in masquerades, where the fabricated hair and decorative attachments may be collected and employed by an antisocial individual to harm the performer. That is why mask performers (among Chokwe-related peoples) are often assisted by someone who collects money but also any loose materials that may fall from the mask.[18] People's coiffures and those attached to masks often include charms for the purpose of counteracting such evil tactics. The charms may protect the wearer but may also "kill" a person who collects it thinking that it could be used against the owner.[19]

Hair may also serve as a form of container for the concealment of other powerful elements.[20] Below layers of hair, the masks of Chokwe and related peoples may include miniature bundles with supernatural attributes. These bundles also serve as charms, but they are meant to appease the ancestor represented through the mask, or the spirit of a previous performer who has passed away. When a mask performer dies, his spirit is said to "reside" in the mask. For a new performer to inherit and perform the same mask, certain rituals are necessary and medicines need to be concealed within the mask to protect him. Bundles underneath mask coiffures often indicate that the mask has been inherited. These bundles may include roots collected from atop the grave of a deceased performer (roots connect "this world" with the world of the ancestor below) and items manufactured in wood or fiber with symbolic meaning. One such symbol is the intertwined fiber spiral, *chijingo*, which denotes an ominous form of transition.[21]

Other Symbolic Associations

The significance of hair as substance or matter is also reflected in ritual performances in which it becomes a symbolic indicator of change or of that which is transitional. In the *mukanda* male initiations of Chokwe-related peoples, it is relatively easy to spot the grandmothers, mothers, and sisters of boys undergoing initiation. During individual rituals and ceremonies that mark important steps toward the conclusion of mukanda, the female relatives often wear highly decorated coiffures with colorful strands of beads and strips of cloth (fig. 105). Some even attach colorful flowers to their hair to indicate their connection and alternative role in the initiation of their sons or relatives. The heavily beaded or decorated hair certainly adds a rattling sound to dances that mark transitional moments in the initiation process. But after hours of continuous dance, fatigue and exhilaration lead to a state in which only the side-to-side motion of the head, and the abrupt shake of the rattling hair, seem to keep the women from entering a total state of trance. In such a case, the decorated hair seems to be part of a ritual psyche or frame of mind.

A direct and highly symbolic association between the mother and her son occurs at the onset of the initiation process. For the actual circumcision of a boy inside the secluded initiation camp, the circumciser first pours water to clean the foreskin and then places it between the palms of his hands, carefully rubbing it to prepare for the

Fig. 105. Photo of a Lunda woman wearing strands of colorful beads on her hair. The beaded coiffure indicates that she is the mother of a boy undergoing a *mukanda* initiation. Photo Manuel Jordán, Zambia, Chitofu Village, 1992.

OPPOSITE
Cat. 136
Face mask
Lwena, Angola
Wood. H: 30.4 cm.
Private Collection

141

Cat. 137
Staff
Ovimbundu, Angola
Wood. H: 49.5 cm.
Roy and Sophia Sieber

Cat. 138
Adze
Ovimbundu, Angola
Wood, glass beads, ceramic,cloth, string.
H: 38.5 cm.
Felix Collection

actual cut. While all this takes place in the privacy of the mukanda initiation camp, at the village the women perform rituals that mimic the preparation of the initiate's foreskin. To do so, the hair of the initiate's mother is lifted above her head and water is poured on it while a female attendant (a relative) rubs her hair back and forth between the palms of her hands. Here, the mother's head and specifically her hair are metaphorically associated with the penis and foreskin of her son.[22] Although the exact meaning of this ritual has not been fully explained, it could be speculated that the regenerative qualities of the mother's hair may reflect hopes for continuity, success, and regeneration (boyhood to manhood) on the part of the initiate.

For the initiates, hair grooming is relevant during two crucial initiation rituals. The initiates' hair is allowed to grow until their circumcision wounds have healed.[23] Then, before a ritual procession, known as *kuliachiza* or *shimba* (among Lunda and Luvale of Zambia), that includes a ritual bath at a river, the initiates get a haircut. This haircut is part of a ritual cleansing that marks their survival of the most dangerous part of initiation, the process of healing, and a fresh start. The initiates' next haircut is on the morning of their graduation, before they return to the village after months in seclusion. At this point the removal of their hair is part of leaving behind the remains of their childhood. The hair that grows from then on is adult hair and part of the graduates' symbolic rebirth into adult life.[24]

Conclusion: Hairstyles versus Art Styles

Because there is at least a general correlation between hairstyles and certain ethnicities, the coiffures depicted in figures and masks may hint at a culture-group association or attribution for an art object. Chokwe figures and masks often include variations of the Chokwe-favored tota or lenge hairstyles. The coiffures, along with known Chokwe scarification details, deeply carved coffee-bean-shaped eyes, and other general conventions of a Chokwe style of carving, should help identify a mask as Chokwe. A mask with "softer" facial features and a larger, rounder, and often deeper coiffure may indicate a Lwena origin (cat. 136). Similarly, figurative items carved to include Ovimbundu-fashion hairstyles (cats. 137, 138) probably indicate an Ovimbundu manufacture. Hairstyles are therefore useful in supporting art-style attributions, particularly if works of art are unaccompanied by field data already providing that information.

As useful as hairstyles may be in suggesting the ethnic identity of individuals or the origins of art objects, they are not infallible because, like art styles and any other elements of good fashion, they are and were often imitated. A degree of prudence is always healthy when making attributions that may seem obvious. Indeed, although certain coiffures may be habitually worn by specific peoples, in some regions it is not uncommon to find a Luluwa woman with a Chokwe hairstyle, a Lunda woman with a Luba coiffure, or a Ngangela woman with a Mwila hairdo.[25] In the case of figurative objects the case may even be more complicated, because carvers often work on commissions from their neighbors.

Fig. 106. The long braids on this Zambian mask help identify it as a representation of *Mwana Pwevo*, or the young woman. Another version of the character, with more abundant "straight" hair is called *Chiwigi*. The name *"Chiwigi"* derives from the English word "wig," referring to the use of modern artificial wigs that are favored by some young women, a commentary on the vanity of female youth. Mize Palace for Luvale Chief Ndungu, Zambia.
Photo: Manuel Jordán, 1997.

Fig. 107. This mask, called *Chiwigi*, is a variation of *the Mwana Pwevo* or "young woman" character. Chitofu Village, Zambia.
Photo: Manuel Jordán, 1992.

For Chokwe-related masquerades, particularly in Zambia and southeastern Angola, hair is an important attribute that helps identify character-types. Certain masks that are constructed from a frame of twigs and branches, to which cloth or tar is applied to model facial details, are almost identical. On these masks it is mainly the coiffure or headdress that serves to identify whether one represents a "powerful male," a "beautiful woman," or an "ambiguous ancestor." Furthermore, although one may identify a specific mask without its hair attached as representative of "the woman," it may be impossible to discern whether the woman in question is adult, young, or older, since different female characters are indicated by different hairstyles (fig. 106, 107).[26]

In regions of Central Africa where elaborate masquerades and diverse figurative carving types and styles may give form to complex cosmological precepts, "hair" may initially seem a superficial subject.[27] But hair comes in layers, and its attributes similarly overlay, from the external and apparent "what it looks like," to ethnicity, and to the "more involved" levels of meaning, supernatural attributes, and symbolic associations. In fact, in its semantic layers, hair in Central Africa is often treated like most sculptural forms, which are created as representational elements that are embellished, treated, or empowered to achieve intended purposes. Hair does matter, then, and, further, more in-depth studies of the complexities of hair will provide more layers of significance.

1. The "related" peoples that I discuss or use in reference for this essay include Chokwe, Lwena, Luvale, Lunda, Luchazi, Mbunda, Ovimbundu, Ngangela, and Mbwela. The "neighbors" include the Mwila, Humbe, Ngambwe, and other ethnicities of southwestern Angola. The information presented here is partially based on field research conducted in Zambia between 1991 and 1993 and in 1997, with generous grants facilitated by the University of Iowa's Project for the Advanced Study of Art and Life in Africa, and by the Birmingham Museum of Art, Alabama.

2. I use 'southern Lunda' here to refer to Lunda groups that reside in Zambia, south of the area of the Lunda (Ruwund or Aruwund) of the Democratic Republic of the Congo, who speak a different language.

3. As explained to me by Henry Kaumba in Zambia while talking about people whose poor physical appearance, including unattended hair, reflected their being 'abandoned' by family and friends.

4. Hairstyles, along with body scarification marks and other forms of body modification (filed teeth, etc.), are still used to identify or 'guess' the ethnic or regional origins of an unknown visitor in areas of Zambia. Problems related to such assumptions are mentioned in the conclusion of this essay.

5. See Bastin (1982:73–75) for a detailed description of Chokwe hairstyles and head adornments.

6. 'Ngangela' is a highly problematic term because it literally means 'people of/from the east,' which is a generic term used by western neighbors to refer to people of different and probably mixed ethnicities who live in central Angola. Eastern neighbors of the 'Ngangela' are the Luchazi, Mbunda, Mbwela, and Chokwe, with whom they share cultural and social traits although their ethnic identity is seemingly distinct. I therefore use 'Ngangela' here for lack of an alternative name. At least one author, Emil Pearson (1977:11–13), reports that the 'VaNgangela' (the prefix 'Va' or 'Ba' means 'people') or 'Ngangela' have accepted either name to fit their common need to be differentiated as long as the prefix 'chi' (ChiNgangela or OchiNgangela) is not used, because it turns the name into a derogatory term. This explanation is necessary because the term has become the source of recent scholarly debate among people who have conducted fieldwork in the neighboring areas.

7. There are numerous alternative spellings for the names of peoples I mention here. For an in-depth ethnographic account of the peoples of southwestern Angola, see Estermann 1983: vols. 1–2.

8. See Cameron 1877, Capello and Ivens 1881, Cardoso 1903, and Carvalho 1896 for examples of accounts that correlate hairstyles with ethnicity.

9. Versions of this hairstyle are commonly replicated as chief's headdresses/crowns. The horned coiffure may metaphorically correlate a chief's power with that of a buffalo or other bovine animal. See Roberts and Maurer 1985:82 for a Central African association between the buffalo and concepts of masculinity. See Roberts 1995 for an excellent study of animal symbolism in African art.

10. These items may also be inserted in the coiffures of masks, and some pins were actually meant to hold the headdresses and crowns of chiefs in place. Bastin (1982:76) reports that wooden combs are worn exclusively by men. I found several decorative combs while conducting fieldwork in Zambia but never saw them being worn. With few exceptions, the majority of wooden combs that were shown to me were kept by men. Almost all of the combs presented to me by men had some form of figurative element in their design. Those kept by women were only decorated with abstract patterns. It is impossible for me to ascertain whether figurative combs are exclusively used by men.

11. This is still true in most areas, where commissioning a work of art comes at great expense for most people. The materials and the degree of elaboration of a piece affect its cost.

12. Hip bustles and leg and arm rattles similarly add sound and 'texture' to these dances. The decorated coiffures are sometimes 'played' by alternating sounds/motions between the head and other parts of the body.

13. The association between hair and concepts of 'life' or 'potency' was explained to me by different Zambian diviners and ritual experts, including Mr. Chitofu Sampoko, Bernard Mukuta Samukinji, Mr. Chipoya, and Mr. Sasombo.

14. This is partly my speculation, although it is consistent with exegetic information provided to me by different Zambian diviners.

15. The term 'medicines' is commonly used in Zambia as a translation of the word *vitumbo*, referring to substances that have particular supernatural powers. There are specific terms for specific 'medicines,' but 'vitumbo' is used when referring to such substances in general terms. Here I make no distinction between 'witchcraft' and 'sorcery.' For an elaboration see Jordán 1996:125–75.

16. As explained to me by Mr. Chitofu Sampoko and Bernard Mukuta Samukinji.

17. The subject of 'love medicines' is rather common knowledge (at least) in areas of northwestern Zambia.

18. These materials may also be used to make someone 'fall in love' against his will. See note 18.

19. That is, if the person collects the 'charm' thinking it is just an ordinary decorative item in the coiffure. However, some of these items are obviously not just decorative (chicken legs, duiker horns, etc.) but are meant to 'advertise' that the person is protected by powerful medicines.

20. For essays elaborating on the subject of secrecy and concealment in African art see Nooter 1993.

21. Manuel L. Rodrigues de Areia (1985:282–93) discusses this symbol in the context of Chokwe divination.

22. My description of the ritual treatment of the mother's hair is based on Elisabeth Cameron's shared knowledge (personal communications 1992, 1997) and on her dissertation (1995), which includes a photograph of the manipulation of a mother's hair at the time of her son's circumcision in Zambia. The latter gives an excellent account of women's roles in the initiations of their sons.

23. This is true of most initiation camps I followed in Zambia from 1991 to 1993 and in 1997. However, there were a few exceptions in *mukanda* camps where the hair of initiates was allowed to grow until the day of graduation.

24. See Felix and Jordán 1998:85–100 for a description of *mukanda* events and their symbolic associations.

25. These are obviously examples but sharing hairstyles is a common practice, particularly if there are no social or political tensions between neighboring ethnicities.

26. It is rather common to find masks without their headdresses or coiffures attached. These items are often removed when pieces are exported from Africa because they may contain animal matter or may be in a state of disrepair, or are not considered an essential aspect of the 'sculpture.'

27. At least to me, initially, as an art historian.

Cross-Dressing for the Spirits in Shambaa *Ughanga*

Barbara THOMPSON

In the Usambara Mountains of northeastern Tanzania, Shambaa healers (*waghanga*) consult with spirit guides through mediumship to learn about healing methods and medicines generally called *ughanga*. Frequently, the healers incorporate characteristic identity-markers of these spirits into their own manner of dress. This enables them to embody their powers. In particular, the healers adorn themselves and their medicine objects, such as gourds, horns, and figurative sculpture, with specific colors and styles that reflect the personal preferences of the spirits. Dressing themselves and their medicine objects in this manner endows them with the ability to divine and heal.

The Shambaa healer Mame Miriamu embodies three spirit guides who permanently coexist in her physical body.[1] One of these spirits is Mphepo Maasai, a Maasai spirit who comes from the savannas surrounding the Usambara Mountains. Since this spirit is a male, specifically a warrior (*olmorani*), Mame Miriamu at all times wears her hair in her own rendition of an *olmorani* hairstyle (fig. 108, see fig. 13). Most Shambaa women wear their hair cropped and covered with a cotton head wrap, but when Mame Miriamu heals under the guidance of Mphepo Maasai, she unties her head wrap to release long strands of braids that tumble out around her head and shoulders. She completes the *olmorani* look by covering her everyday garments with red and white cloth, accentuated by beaded necklaces and bracelets. Mame Miriamu also incorporates additional icons of Maasai identity into her work, including a locally made spear similar to those used by Maasai warriors, and a medicine gourd (*nkhoba*) decorated with beadwork in Maasai colors. When she is not healing with the aid of Mphepo Maasai, Mame Miriamu hides her hairstyle under her head wrap, disguising her embodied male Maasai identity under the appearance of a typical Shambaa woman.

Mame Miriamu notes that spirits, like humans, have personal preferences, gender, ethnic identity, and family relationships (spirit spouses and children). They also have ranks and responsibilities within the spirit world (Miriamu, personal communication, March 18, 1998). If the spirits are to cooperate with humans, it is important

Fig. 108. The Shambaa healer Mame Miriamu reveals her *Mphepo Maasai* hairstyle while displaying other medicine objects embodying the warrior spirit, including a spear, a beaded medicine gourd (*nkhoba*), and white beaded necklaces crossed over her chest. Lushoto District, Tanzania.
Photo: Barbara Thompson, 1998.

147

that the healer respect their individuality and honor them by dressing in their own specific manner. In order to maintain a positive working relationship with Mphepo Maasai, Mame Miriamu must transform her own Shambaa identity—while remaining, of course, within the permissible boundaries of being a Shambaa female—to embody her male spirit's *olmorani* identity and individual preferences. "All things Mphepo Maasai likes relate to his Maasai ethnicity. If I do not do these things for Mphepo Maasai, then I will get sick . . . and he will not help me in healing my patients" (Miriamu, personal communication, March 18, 1998). By dressing herself, her hair, and her symbolic healing objects in a Maasai manner, Mame Miriamu invites the Maasai spirit to "move" with her and aid her in healing (Miriamu, personal communication, March 18, 1998).

This essay is based on fieldwork conducted in northeastern Tanzania in the summer of 1996 and from May 1997 to May 1998. The research was generously supported by the University of Iowa Program for the Advanced Study of Art and Life in Africa (P.A.S.A.L.A.), The University of Iowa Graduate College, The Kress Foundation, and The Stanley Foundation.

1. The term *mame* means "mother" in the Shambaa language and is used as a title to address a senior woman.

A Note on Gender Reversal

Gender reversal, even transvestitism, exists elsewhere in Africa, although it has been little studied. For instance, as Babatunde Lawal notes, male devotees (priests) are considered to be the wives of the *orisas* (deities) and at ceremonies are costumed and coiffed as women. Otherwise they live normal Yoruba lives but must not marry female devotees of the same orisa (Frank Speed, personal communication, 1971).

According to Battel (1613), the men of the Benguela Kingdom "are beastley in their living, for they have men in Womens Apparel, whom they keep amongst their Wives" (Astley III:273).

Writing in 1676, Olfert Dapper recorded that the self-declared Queen of Angola, Xinga, had assumed the role of king in the 1640s:

> *As she went in Man's Habit, she assumed a Man's Name, and her Gallants, who were cloathed in Womens Apparel, took the Name of Females; giving-out, that they were Women, and she a Man: Nor dared her Favourites say the contrary, on Pain of losing their Heads: On the other Hand, as a Mark of her confidence, she permitted them the Freedom to converse with her Women (Dapper, in Astley III:280).* [R.S.]

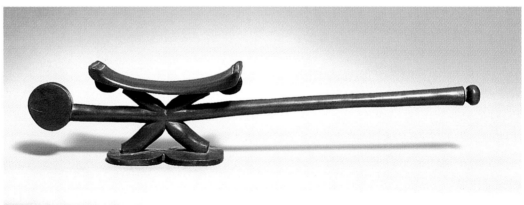

Cat. 139
Headrest
Nguni, South Africa
Wood. L: 55.9 cm.
Kevin Conru

Cat. 140
Neckrest
Nguni, South Africa
Wood. H: 14 cm.
Mr. and Mrs. Donald Morris

Headrests and Hairpins
Signifying More Than Status

Karel NEL

Headrests

A headrest, carried above the heads of the crowd, surges forward as the celebrating group leaves the homestead of the bride's father. This departure marks the start of a journey across the hills to the homestead of her new husband. She leaves her familial homestead with apprehension, about to take on her new role as a wife, carrying with her the honor, pride, traditions, and skills of her family. Soon she will be expected to adapt and fit into the unfamiliar patterns and routines of her husband's family. At first a relative outsider and a junior in a patriarchal society, her importance, her value as a wife, and her full acceptance into her new family will only be conferred at the birth of her first child. C. Hamilton has remarked that "they become outsiders in their marital contexts and inhabit multiple social margins as women, young brides and outsiders in patriarchal, age-governed and lineage-organized settings" (Hamilton 1998:25).

The headrest that travels with the bride cannot be viewed as a mere object—as we see it reproduced in books, or in isolated displays in this exhibition. It is carried on a tide of emotion and belief, a nexus for intersecting values and a focus of expectations. First of all, as a part of her dowry, the headrest is a betrothal object, commissioned by the young bride for her new husband from a specialist carver. (In the past, the carver would always have been a man, for in southern Africa the working of different materials was gender-specific: only men carved wood, while women would work with beads, cloth, and clay. This gender division in the use of material has eroded somewhat in more recent times.)

Sleeping with a headrest signifies the young couple's change of status, for unmarried people sleep without one. There are examples of paired headrests that seem to have been commissioned for both members of the newly married couple. The head-

Fig. 109. *Zulu Ntimba* or bridal party en route to a wedding, bride is behind man wearing a white turban, Zululand? *Photo: Lynn Acutt, 1930s to 1950s. By kind permission, Ken Karner.*

rest is also a necessity at the point of marriage, because the new status of both the bride and the groom will be manifested through the adoption of elaborate hairstyles.

Married women's hairstyles have differed greatly both regionally and historically throughout Africa, but were universally quite elaborate. Among the Zulu, for example, the word *ihloko*—meaning the point of a sharp or tapering object, and also, by extension, the head—has generally been used to describe married women's hairstyles, and accurately describes the tapering and pointed coiffure of an earlier period, often to be seen in older figurative carvings and historical photographs. The forms that these hairstyles subsequently took were often regional. In the area north of the Thukela in KwaZulu-Natal, South Africa, for example, a cylindrical form was favored and is still in use, whereas in the Msinga area not far away, married women adopt a style that flares outward from the head. The upper perimeter of the style is closed off as a large flat disk. Another style has also found favor in Msinga: the hair is gathered into two separate elongated cones stretching out above the woman's ears (Klopper 1992:139). Political and historical pressures lead to differentiation of one group from another. Through the adoption of particular hairstyles, the groups attempted to differentiate themselves clearly one from another.

These traditional styles are constructed around a framework of reeds, grass, and cloth, which is attached by stitching the hair into the framework and thereby securing it firmly to the head (Bryant 1949:153). The hair around the periphery of the hairstyle is pulled over the framework and tied at the top. Once in place, the hairstyle is rubbed with animal fat and colored a deep or brilliant red with ocher, a substance with powerful symbolic resonances associated with rituals of liminality. The construction of such coiffures is extraordinarily time-consuming, and the structure could easily be crushed out of shape by a single night's unsupported sleep, so the headrest is crucial for maintaining this dramatic artifice.

In the past, the Zulu groom could have had conferred upon him by the king the right to wear the prized headring called the *isicoco* (Klopper 1992:138). A special

Cat. 141
Headrest
Zulu, South Africa
Wood. H: 17.1 cm.
Drs. Jean and Noble Endicott

craftsman would secure this oval framework of palm fibers to the head by sewing the hair around it and binding it with string or tendon. It was then coated with a natural latex, which was polished to attain a luster (Bryant 1949:143). Once completed, the isicoco appeared as a burnished oval ring on the crown of the head, while the surrounding scalp was clean shaven. This precious sign of status was also protected by sleeping on a headrest, where the support was either to neck or cheek, thus ensuring that no undue pressure was placed on the attachment.

The Zulu and Swazi peoples, who are generally grouped together under the broader category Nguni, are represented on the show by three fine large headrests. Zulu and Swazi headrests tend to be rectangular in shape, with a broad, slightly concave upper surface that acquires beautiful translucent patinas through years of use.

The largest of these three is ambiguous in its nature: while it takes the form of a headrest, its scale is closer to that of a stool (cat. 139). The piece is characterized by a series of extravagant loops that function either as handles or legs. The sumptuous complexity of the design is reminiscent of certain large vessels generally attributed to Swazi craftsmen, though this connection remains conjecture. The piece reflects the practice, noticeable in southern African pieces, of playing off virtuosity against sheer simplicity of geometric form.

The elegant curved upper platform of the Zulu headrest (cat. 141) is supported by a pair of monumental columns on either side of an arch compressed between them. The play between the chamfered surfaces of the columns and the spaces created between them reveals a honed aesthetic, alerting the viewer to the fact that this is not merely a simple household object but one of greater significance.

Created and put into use at the beginning of a marriage, a headrest accretes a lifetime of associations, becoming intimately bound to the identity of the owner. For this reason it is often buried with the body of the person who used it. Alternatively the headrest may be bequeathed to a daughter, who, in time, will give it to her husband. Such a gift weaves together clans and generations, connecting the bride's husband

Cat. 142
Neckrest
Ngoni, Tanzania
Wood. H: 14.6 cm.
Drs. Jean and Noble Endicott

with her father as a symbol of the continuity of the lineage. If the headrest is not buried, it may be used as a means of accessing the *amadlozi* (guardian spirits) or the *idlozi*, the spirit of the particular forefather. This may be achieved through the dream state while sleeping on the headrest, or the headrest can be used by ritual healers, *inyangas* or *sangomas*, to access the ancestors during consultations.

The third of the headrests is unusual in its overt resemblance to a bull (cat. 142). Most Swazi headrests are more covert in their reference. The upper surface of this headrest sags between the pairs of legs, like the belly of a bull. The lower curve is punctuated by a central protuberance, associated both with the umbilicus and the penis of the bull. In this unusual example the two ends are much more representative of the head of the bull than is usual. In most cases the ends become symmetrical and reduced, as stylized heads or tails. Headrests of this type never appear to represent a single animal—the fact that the ends are always identical suggests either two animals side-by-side but facing in opposite directions, or two animals conjoined at the umbilicus. This understanding seems consonant with S. Klopper's observation that in many Nguni headrests the numerous pairs of legs were probably intended to evoke the idea of a large herd. The reference to cattle is entirely understandable given that cattle are a major source of wealth, and it is through them that people maintain communication with their ancestors (Klopper 1995:207–8).

The fact that the headrest given by the bride to her husband alludes to cattle should come as no surprise, for the bridegroom's family will have given the bride's family a gift of cattle by way of recognition of her worth and in thanks for their generosity. This gift, called *lobola*, was considered primarily as sealing an alliance between two families. The cattle involved were regarded as "the knot of relationship and marriage, therefore when a girl goes to one kraal, something is to go from that kraal to the father of the girl, so that each family should possess something."

Without the binding formality of the gift of cattle, there was no legitimacy to a marriage; women considered the marriage incomplete and themselves vulnerable (Mostert 1992:963–64). The headrest, with its allusion to the bride-wealth cattle that have allied the families, symbolically refers to that conjunction. It also looks both forward into the future, in terms of the children who will be born from this union, and ultimately backward to the forebears from whom the couple came.

The single Shona headrest on show would have originated in present-day Zimbabwe (cat. 143) . It is significantly smaller than the examples already discussed, and markedly different in its whole gestalt. The primary shape for the Shona headrest is a square. These headrests are markedly narrower than the Nguni versions, and the primary metaphor underpinning the form is not male and animal but female and human. No less than the Nguni headrests, the Shona headrests are the focus of a network of ideas and symbols, but rather different ones—though nonetheless related to the ancestors, the birth of children, and wealth and status.

Cat. 143
Neckrest
Shona, Zimbabwe
Wood. H: 13.3 cm.
Marc and Denyse Ginzberg Collection

The bases of Shona headrests frequently consist of two lobes that adjoin in such a way as to form a small triangle between them, rather as the female pubis lies between the legs. Sometimes this allusion is quite abstract, but some examples are quite explicit. The same imagery occurs even when the base consists of three lobes. A. Nettleton has written, "When a man slept and dreamed he was said to be visiting his ancestors, the source of knowledge and prosperity. The headrests as female figures without heads further amplify this ancestral connection. When a man marries a woman the Shona say that he owns her body but that her head (i.e. the seat of her ancestral 'being') belongs always to her father" (1995:204).

The resting surface of Shona headrests is elegantly concave, and is sometimes embellished with precisely engraved zigzag or triangular motifs. These may be carved either on the ends or across the entire curved upper surface. This surface is often ever so slightly angled downward on the one long side; knowledgeably crafted for its purpose, it ensures maximum comfort for the sleeper.

The central section of the headrest, which joins the base to the resting surface, is invariably planar. Deeply incised circular and triangular motifs combine with the spaces between them to form this thin vertical slab. These motifs are put together in a variety of elegant patterns, based on either two, three, or six circles sandwiched between rows of triangles or zigzags. When this central section is developed around two disks, this configuration seems to allude to female breasts, and in some cases is carved as such. Frequently, though, the disks are deeply incised with a series of concentric circles around a small central boss. Multivalent in Shona iconography, this image refers to the fact that the ancestral realm was visualized as a sacred pool, as indeed was a woman's womb (Nettleton 1995:204). As much as these disks represent breasts, so too could they represent the womb as a site of generative power. Another interpretation of this motif has been the ripples made in the pool after a stone has been thrown into it—a means of alerting the ancestors that their attention is required. It may also be that the image of the stone being thrown into the pool symbolizes the conception of a child—and the continuation of a lineage.

As has already been intimated, headrests moved from one village to another, and from region to region. In addition, anyone traveling would probably take with them their sleeping mat and headrest, as can be seen in Blaise Junod's photograph of a Swazi traveler (Junod 1938:frontispiece, fig. 110). Evidence of the fact that these important personal objects were taken along when people traveled has come in the form of headrests found far afield from their area of origin—Shona headrests in Mpumalanga, on the border of KwaZulu-Natal, and headrests of Tsonga origin well into modern-day Zimbabwe.

Indeed some headrests were designed as traveling headrests as can be seen in a striking piece that combines headrest with ceremonial stick (cat. 140). The unusual conjunction of headrest and stick into a single object has been done in such a way as to combine beauty with function, since the traveler would be required to take both along with him.

A simple, single stick, characteristically minimal in its clarity of form, was traditionally presented to every young man on his attainment of manhood after initiation, and was a symbol of his new standing. The stick became closely identified with its

Fig. 110. Swazi traveler with sleeping mat and headrest.
Photo: Blaise Junod, 1938.

Cat. 144
Neckrest
East Africa
Wood, fiber, metal. H: 15.9 cm.
Marc and Denyse Ginzberg Collection

Cat. 145
Neckrest
Bari, Sudan
Wood, leather. H: 12.7 cm.
Roy and Sophia Sieber

Cat. 146
Neckrest
East Africa
Wood, leather. H: 16.5 cm.
Roy and Sophia Sieber

owner and came to represent his presence. He would always carry the stick on important ceremonial occasions and when he visited or traveled. A man would also leave his stick at the entrance of his home to indicate his presence.

A big disk forms the head of this stick/headrest, and its cylindrical shaft passes through the headrest's long axis. The headrest itself consists of three elements—a flattened, double-lobed base, a central section made of two abutting C-shaped forms, and surmounting the latter a highly polished resting surface, which has a pair of lugs extending downward. On some headrests, lugs such as these are adorned with beads and wildebeest hair out of respect for the ancestors. Such headrests are said to be "dressed," suggesting that the headrest, though seemingly abstract, is actually somewhat anthropomorphic.

The central section of this headrest, which consists of two, bold arrowlike elements, is penetrated at the point of juncture by the shaft of the stick. All of these elements are markedly volumetric in their carving, a feature distinguishing the object from the relieflike quality of Shona carving. This central section, with its dramatic extensions to left and right, breaks the conventional boundaries associated with the form of the headrest.

This headrest, and others similar to it, have generally been ascribed to Tsonga/Shangaan carvers, but R. Becker asserts that attributing historical headrests to modern ethnic groupings such as the Tsonga or Shangaan is problematic, and that a regional grouping would be more plausible (1995:206). For this piece the region of origin would most probably include parts of present day Zimbabwe, southern Mozambique, and the eastern part of the Northern Province of South Africa.

Although the number of headrests in the exhibition is limited, they do indicate how widespread the custom of making and using headrests was in Africa. The examples on show come chiefly from the southern African region and include fine pieces

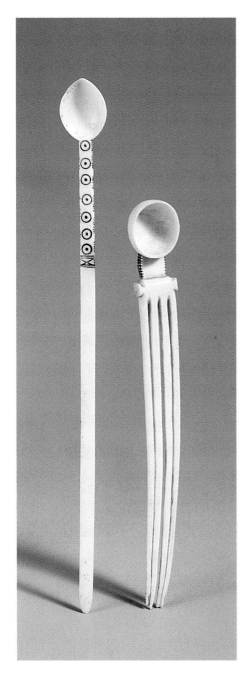

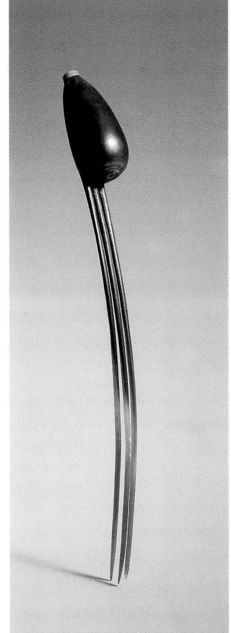

Cat. 147
Hairpin/ spoon
Zulu, South Africa
Ivory. H: 19.4 and 14.6 cm.
Marc and Denyse Ginzberg Collection

Cat. 148
Hairpin/snuff container
Zulu, South Africa
Horn, metal. H: 26.7 cm.
Marc and Denyse Ginzberg Collection

Fig. 111. Bhaca woman with snuff
spoons in her hair.
Photo: N.J. Van Warmelo, 1948.

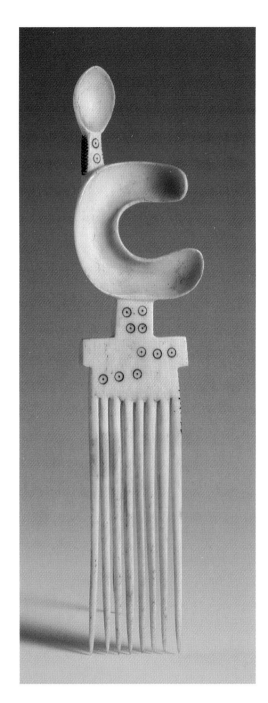

Cat. 149
Comb
East Africa or Zulu, South Africa
Ivory. H: 17.6 cm.
Etnografisch Museum, Antwerp;
Gift M. Olbrechts (1977)

from the Nguni (Zulu/Swazi), the Tsonga/Shangaan, and the Shona. The other headrests are from other parts of Africa—Tanzania on the East Coast, Sudan, and a single example from the Himba, a migratory group in the harsh, dry desert areas of the west coast of northern Namibia (cats. 144, 146).

When one sees these pieces displayed together, it becomes clear that much work still needs to be done in order to understand the huge historic web of how and where headrests emerged in deep time, and how they evolved stylistically and structurally, creating specific tendencies that have manifested themselves over vast regions. There are startling similarities among headrests from places far apart, as well as differences among headrests made by craftsmen in relatively close proximity to one another. The intriguing questions are inevitably whether headrests evolved spontaneously from a specific need, which might have arisen out of a widespread practice of elaborate hairstyling all over the continent, or whether the idea traveled with specific cultural and historical migrations over extended periods of time.

The complex and varied styling of hair across the African continent codified shifts in status relative to the living members of a person's society as well as to his or her forebears. In societies with a high degree of consonance between these two realms, the dressing of hair inevitably reflected both the present social realm and that of the spirit world. It comes as little surprise, then, that many of the hair ornaments on display have a strong relationship to the taking and sharing of snuff, a substance connected to the ancestral realm.

Tobacco and its inhalable form, snuff, were once scarce and valuable commodities, and sharing them would have been read as a sign of one's wealth and generosity. The heightened sensations created by taking snuff were also associated with access to the ancestral world, thus unifying the social and the spiritual in a single act of social communion. It seems that the inhalation of substances such as snuff serves to heighten the perception of sensations, including sexual ones, and snuff was therefore also associated with both virility and fecundity.

In southern Africa, snuff was generally stored in small portable containers that were carried about in some unusual ways: pushed through a pierced and enlarged hole in the lobe of an ear, hung as a pendant around the neck, or included in some larger form of beaded decoration. The snuff container even occasionally became part of a long comb that could be stuck jauntily through the hair. The fine example on view (cat. 148), carved from a single horn, combines the classic teardrop-shaped container with three long prongs. The piece is remarkable in being simultaneously extraordinarily restrained and uncommonly showy.

The three snuff spoons on display move from the simply spoonlike to the distinctively comblike (cats. 147, 149). Even in the case of the snuff spoon proper, all of these would have functioned as hair adornments. That snuff spoons were put to ornamental use can be seen in a 1948 photograph of a young Bhaca woman from the Mount Frere district, Eastern Cape, South Africa (Shaw & Van Warmelo 1988:755) (fig. 111). Such a young woman must surely have been very sociable—and well-connected with the ancestors.

The most comblike of these spoons is also the least spoonlike, being a combination of two or possibly even three spoons, depending on how one thinks about it:

the ornamental part of the comb is made up of an unusual C-shaped bowl, designed to be placed under the nose with the two ends precisely below the two nostrils, enabling its user to sniff the snuff up both nostrils simultaneously (rather than alternately, as was usually the case). Furthermore, the C-shaped spoon is surmounted by another small, conventionally shaped spoon, making this a rather extravagant object as it playfully transforms itself from comb to hair decoration, to double snuff spoon, and finally culminates in an elegant finial that is also a spoon.

While there are beautiful examples of hairpins made of bone, horn or ivory, where there is no intention beyond ornamentation, it is clear from this sample of hair ornaments that some served purposes in addition to pure adornment. By integrating the accouterments of social interaction—the snuffbox and spoons—with hair ornaments, the wearer, unencumbered, was able to take along the means of enhancing social intercourse. These signaled his or her social standing while at the same time signifying potential access to the spirit realm.

Cat. 150
Headrest
Luba, Shankadi, Democratic Republic of
Congo
Wood, beads, fiber. H: 16 cm.
Corice and Armand P. Arman

Neckrests

Neckrests (often called headrests or pillows) have been used all over the African continent. They are found as part of the grave furniture of ancient Egypt and Nubia. The concept may have traveled from the north throughout the continent, but it is by no means impossible that the move was from south to north in prehistoric times. The variety of forms does suggest that the idea is very old and that its many formal manifestations are the result of long separate evolutions. [R.S.]

Fig. 112. Two women with cascade coiffures, Luba, Democratic Republic of Congo.
Photo: Franck, first half 20th century.

Cat. 151
Headrest
Luba, Democratic Republic of Congo
Wood. H: 17 cm.
Private Collection

Cat. 152
Neckrest
Mfinu, Democratic Republic of Congo
Wood. H: 15.8 cm.
Private Collection

Cat. 153
Neckrest
Yaka, Democratic Republic of Congo
Wood. H: 16.5 cm.
Private Collection

Cat. 154
Neckrest
Yaka, Democratic Republic of Congo
Wood. H: 14.3 cm.
Private Collection

Cat. 155
Neckrest
Kuba, Democratic Republic of Congo
Wood. H: 16.5 cm.
Pamela and Oliver E. Cobb

Cat. 156
Neckrest
Rendile, East Africa
Wood. H: 17.1 cm.
Mona Gavigan/Affrica

Rasta Hair, U.S. and Ghana: A Personal Note

Mariama ROSS

Hair, the crowning glory of women down through the ages, makes statements about the wearer in the same way her clothing speaks of who she is. As fashion trends influence clothing worn by women, so does it determine, to a large extent, how they wear their hair. Within the boundaries of current fashion, a woman's hairstyle can also convey information about her age, socio-economic or marital status, education, and politics. Certainly, it tells a lot about her concept of herself, either as who she is or who she wants to be. Her choice of hairstyle is also a reflection of societal and cultural norms which she either adheres to or rejects. I spent the summer of 1999 doing dissertation research in Ghana, West Africa, and one of the things I experienced there was the clash of cultures around the issue of hair.

Hairstyles in African American Society

My hair was, and is, worn in a style now fairly common in the U.S. I have shoulder-length dreadlocks. Although I have heard that dread locks have their origins in ancient Egypt, my earliest memory of seeing this style was in the 1960's on the late Jamaican reggae musician, Bob Marley, who had waist-length locks. The style has spread since then and is now worn by African American women and men of Jamaican and Rastafarian extraction, those who are not from Jamaican or Rastafarian. The latter group can be found living in major metropolitan cities and at all levels of education and socio-economic status, and whose political opinions are decidedly left of center. I have never seen the style worn by politically conservative individuals. It has been somewhat legitimized, or at least familiarized, by literary and political luminaries Toni Morrison, Angela Davis, and Alice Walker. Because it is a "natural" hairstyle, that is, unstraightened, it appeals to people who eschew processes of mechanical or chemical straightening. Relatedly, locks are commonly worn by those of us who, coming out of the 60's and 70's age of the "Afro," continue to prefer making the revolutionary and "in your face" political statements with our hair that began in that era.

Hairstyles in Ghana—Summer of '99

In May, 1999 I arrived in Ghana to do research on art and popular culture. On a short trip in 1997 I had seen the hairstyles there and knew that many urban women wore short straightened coiffures, some sported braided extensions, and some wore close-cropped natural do's. In 1999 I was surprised to find almost exclusively straight hair on women over the age of nineteen or so, and a proliferation of women wearing extensions. I saw almost no natural hair on adult women in cities. Most secondary schools still require short-cropped natural hair as part of the uniform dress code, presumably because it is supposed to give one a youthful, innocent, less sophisticated appearance. Billboards and TV commercials advertise hair straightening products with long swinging hair-styles worn by thin models in short, tight clothing. Just like in the States, the clear message was that straight "wind-blown" hair will make women sexy, desirable, and popular. Braided extensions are now extremely popular amongst urban Ghanaian women. On a bus ride from Accra to Kumasi, of the total twenty-two women aboard, thirteen had extensions, and eight had straightened hair. I was the only one with natural hair.

My Hair in Ghana

Having been in Ghana for five weeks in 1997, I knew that my hair attracts attention and distinguishes me beyond my obvious foreigner or "obruni" appearance. I was accustomed to having people call to me from across the street, waving and shouting a friendly greeting of "Rasta!" I would usually wave back, acknowledging the greeting, despite not being "rasta," at least in my own eyes.

My second trip was more extended, allowing me to live with Ghanaians and interact with them much more than I had earlier. In my many conversations with individuals encountered in and around my house, during social engagements, and in the interviews I was conducting for my research, people often asked my about my hair. Despite the African convention of verbal indirection, I found these Ghanaians to be very direct in their curiosity about my locks. The question, often coming out of the blue, was usually as blunt as, "Why do you wear your hair like that?" I learned that to respond to that simple question with a simple answer such as, "I like it this way," did not suffice. What they were asking was much more complex and was based on their knowledge of people who wear locks. In their experience, locks are part of the garb of fetish priests and priestesses, whose hair gets that way as a result of their mysterious dealing with the spirit world. They know also that Rastafarians from Jamaica wear their hair this way. Despite liking reggae music produced by those folks, none of the people I spoke with had ever had anything to do with Rastafari and knew nothing about them. since I did not fit either profile, they did not understand who I was. Through direct and indirect probing I learned that to them my kind of hair was associated with restricted substances and the state of being unwashed, frightening, mysterious, and forbidden. Many times I would attempt to counter their reluctance to believe I was anything but a Rastafarian by saying that I define my self basically as a Christian. On one such occasion the young man looked at me quizzically and asked, "Are you sure?"

There were a number of times when an actual Rastafarian, thinking me a kinswoman, would attempt to engage me in conversation. My inability to engage in discourse about Ja, I and I, or even reggae music made them look at me with what appeared to be either sympathy or disdain.

While I found these encounters amusing for the most part, they do speak of the complex connections and dis-connects between Africans throughout the Diaspora. They hint at the myriad layers of cultural perceptions and misperceptions between Africa and the West that must be mined with care, sensitivity, and much time. Additionally, like other aspects of popular culture, hairstyles, if viewed contextually, can yield much information about cultural borrowing and re-interpretation.

Cat. 157
Kiosk for a barber shop with contents
Ghana.
Wood, metal roofing sheets, wire mesh,
vinyl sheet flooring, enamel paint.
213.4 x 213.4 x 213.4 cm.
Ernie Wolfe Gallery, Los Angeles

OPPOSITE
Cat. 158
Barber shop sign
Ghana
Enamel on wood panel. H: 45.8 cm.
Private Collection

Contemporary Africa

The styling of hair in contemporary Africa reflects both innovations and borrowings as well as a commitment to old forms and techniques. To visit an African urban center is to be exposed to a delightful passing parade of the rich variety of contemporary styles.

[R.S.]

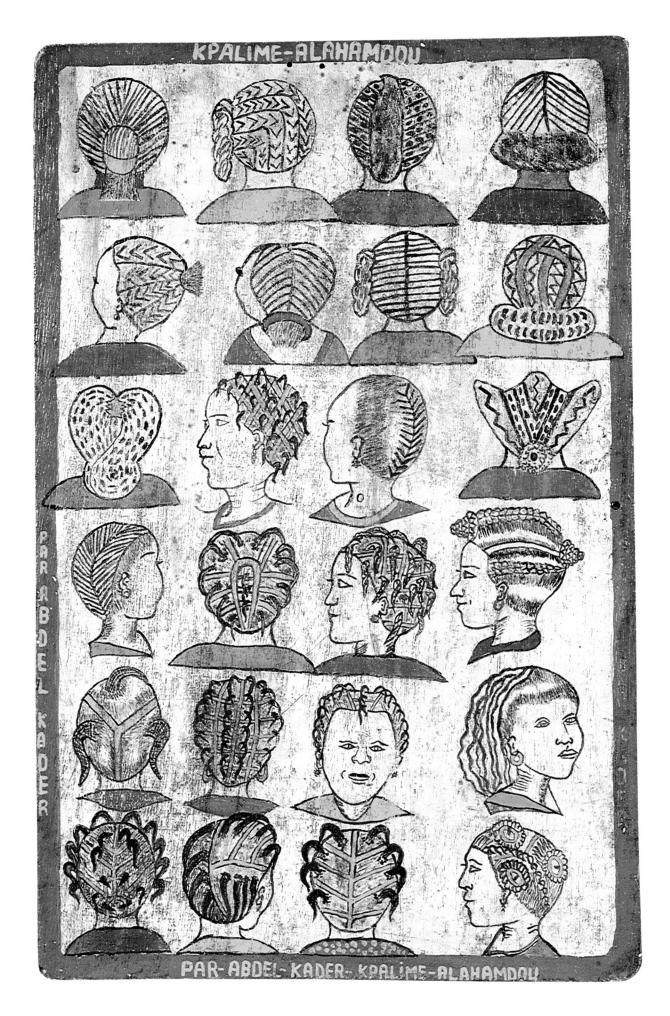

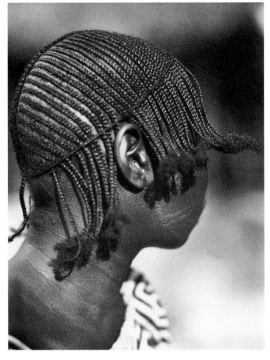

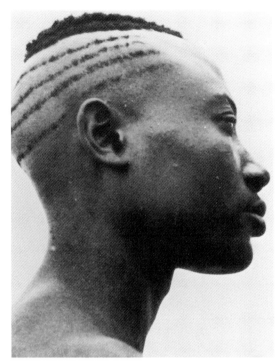

Fig. 113. Coiffure, province of the Equator, Democratic Republic of Congo.
Photo: Zagourski, 1926-1937.

Fig. 114. Man's hairstyle designed according to personal taste, Wambo, Namibia.
Photo: K. Schettler (Archiv Scherz), 1940s.

Fig. 115. Galla man (now Oromo), Sudan.
Photo: Zagourski, 1926-1937.

Fig. 116. Children, unknown provenance.
Photo: Afrika Museum, Berg en Dal.

OPPOSITE
Cat. 159
Barber Shop sign
West Africa
Enamel on wood panel. H: 61 cm.
Roy and Sophia Sieber

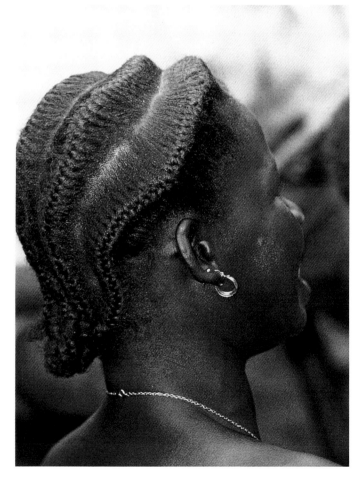

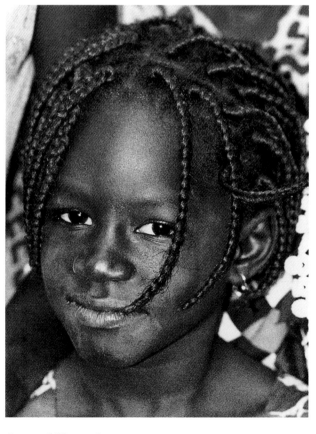

Fig. 117. Children and women,
Burkina Faso.
Photos: Robert Rubin, 1999.

Cat. 160
Barber shop sign
Ghana
Enamel on wood panel. H: 74.3 cm.
Private Collection

Cat. 161
Barber shop sign
Ghana
Enamel on wood panel. H: 59.9 cm.
Private Collection

Cat. 162
Barber shop sign
Ghana
Enamel on wood panel. H: 60.5 cm.
Private Collection

What Is *Really* Happening Here? Black Hair among African-Americans and in American Culture

Kennell JACKSON

Midway through the 1999 NBA playoffs, AND 1, a basketball apparel company, broadcast an eye-catching ad featuring the controversial New York Knicks player Latrell Sprewell, who was at that moment the playoffs' star. Viewers first saw his name in capitals, next his face, then his unfurled, towering crown of hair. Once the camera pulled back, he was seen sitting on the floor as a woman braided his hair.

When the camera returned to Latrell's face, he delivered a soliloquy that began, "I know I have made mistakes," and ended, "People say I am basketball's worst nightmare. But I say I am the American Dream." The last shot showed Latrell transformed: his hair was now in neat zigzagging rows, a little masterpiece of symmetries, a kind of cubism. He had become "Spree," his public self, whose braids are seen by his fans as symbolizing his freedom. Accenting this freedom on the soundtrack was Jimmy Hendrix's iconoclastic version of "The Star Spangled Banner." Although the ad lasted a mere thirty seconds, it was total spectacle.

People talked about this ad, specifically about its hair revelations. The ad took us into an interior African-American cultural moment—a hair-braiding ritual, one usually reserved for family and friends, where the crafting of hair is spiced by banter and gossip. Revealed also was the women's art form behind Lattrell's mannish public persona. But some viewers were startled by the revelation of his massive unfurled hair. Later, on talk radio, someone asked, "Is that what his hair is really like? Is black hair like that?"

The Prevalence of the "Black Hair Event" in Recent America

The unveiling of "Latrell braids" constituted what could be called a "black hair event" or a "black hair moment," one of those moments that occur when the hair of African-Americans grabs America's attention. These moments are often quite fleeting, like the public's infatuation with Don King's electrified coiffure. But sometimes they last for years, as with the rise of braiding styles. Ultimately these moments reflect our culture's fascination, indeed obsession—shared by both blacks and nonblacks—with black hair.

OPPOSITE
Cat. 163
Barber shop sign
Ghana
Enamel on wood. H: 47.6 cm.
Drs. Jean and Noble Endicott

Of late these events have become common-place. "Hairesies," a 1997 SoHo art show by Alison Saar, devoted to black hair, became a hot-ticket item. Ada Babino got a lot of attention for her docudrama *Middle Passage-N-Roots*, a look at the cultural baggage blacks carry on top of their heads. Using Carolivia Herron's children's book *Nappy Hair* (1997) in a Brooklyn third-grade class provoked such a howl that the august *New York Times* ran an editorial on it; both the protest and editorial qualify as black hair events. Singer Brandi "made history" by being on the cover of *Seventeen* wearing braids. Another first was *W*'s ranking of black hairstyles among "Fashion's 100 Greatest Moments."

Today's television revels in black hair. The comedian Sinbad has deconstructed the hair anxieties of blacks. *Living Single* had an episode on dreadlocks in the workplace. The style Aretha Franklin wore when she appeared on *Oprah*—high, polished flat curls—was reviewed. Music videos achieve buzz through new hairstyles.

Then there are the ad hair events. In the mid-1990s, Coca-Cola used a black barbershop as an ad backdrop. Then McDonald's used Patti Labelle's flamboyant hair to sell Big Macs. Recently the telephone company Sprint aired a witty ad about a black student trying to get a haircut from a white barber. (The barber gets instructions from the student's inner-city barber, by—you guessed it!—a phone call.) In 1999 alone, ads for ATT, Suretrade.com, TransAmerica, Yahoo, Gap, and K-Mart delved into black hair. TVLand advertises its offerings with a brown-skinned Fred Murray sporting tiny dreadlocks, and saying "Times Change. Great TV Doesn't."

As Richard Pryor used to say, "What is *really* happening here? Did anyone expect *this*?" Is the hair of African-Americans becoming dramatically more visible? Is this hair—long the butt of stereotypes, long a source of anxiety within black society, long subordinated to an idealized Euro-American hair (often depicted in ads as lengthy, straight, blonde, and permanently in luxurious slow motion)—acquiring new stature? Is it also finally becoming accepted, even understood? Paraphrasing Rodney King's question, "Is all our hair finally going to get along?"

Probably not. Prejudice still stalks black hair. From high schools to corporate America, wearing huge Afro wigs to taunt blacks is the bigot's new weapon of choice. Still, we could be entering a new accommodationist phase for black hair in America—a new hair moment. How did we get to this situation? What caused the new visibility?

Fig. 119. Brooklyn, 1983.
Photo: Chester Higgins, Jr.

OPPOSITE
Fig. 118. "Mahema," Zimbabwe, 1996.
Photo: Chester Higgins, Jr.

Fig. 120. Senegal, 1991.
Photo: Chester Higgins, Jr.

The Afro Event: The First Major Visbility

If there was ever a black hair event, it was the ascendance of the Afro hairstyle in the 1960s. So important was the Afro that poet Sonia Sanchez started her famous poem "we a baddDDD people" with,

> I mean,
>
> > we bees real
>
> bad.
> > we gots bad songs
> sung on every station
> we gots some bad NATURALS
> on our heads...

She got the moment's meaning right. The Afro was deemed "bad," definitely different, threatening, and it was socially and aesthetically disruptive for America and for African-Americans. "Militant" was inscribed on the Afro. Afro-wearers were the 1960s *sans-culottes.*

Evidence now shows that the Afro—also called the "natural" and the "fro" by the hip—was germinating as early as the mid-1950s. Its earliest wearers were a motley, scattered group: actors and actresses, a new breed of designers and models, musicians, college students, Africa-travelers, working class activists, Chicago and Detroit gang members, Oakland and Los Angeles youth, and black nationalists. In a sense, these fragments coalesced to become the vanguard intelligentsia of the Afro. They constructed and proclaimed its single-minded message, namely the repudiation of the half-century of straightened hair among blacks. By 1959, the Afro was gaining ground among blacks, a clue being its endorsement in Lorraine Hansberry's play *A Raisin in the Sun*. Its almost-complete sweep was reflected in the election, in October 1966, of Afro-wearing Robin Gregory to be Howard University's homecoming queen, a sensation for that black middle-class citadel.

Within Black America, the movement toward the Afro embraced a variety of submovements. The hairstyle represented much: a passion for things African (clothing, art, language, especially Swahili); an anti-assimilationist and anti-integrationist movement; a young peoples' revolt, later cresting in "Black Power" politics; and a debate about cultural authenticity. Lastly, it represented the inherent restlessness of fashion. Black fashion in the twentieth century has waited for no one.

The impact of the natural was not confined to black America. Soon it was a major icon across the visual landscape of America. Who, of a certain age, doesn't remember photographs of celebrity Afro-coiffed blacks: Margaret Burroughs, Odetta, Black Panthers, Muhammad Ali, the Staple Singers, Ishmael Reed, Misses Black America, Jesse Jackson, Gwendolyn Brooks, and of course Tamara Dobson and Pam Grier, whose Afros seemed to

Fig. 121. "Lew-Eleanor, Knots," New York City, 1998.
Photo: Chester Higgins, Jr.

empower their kick-ass film tactics? Easily remembered also is the cross-cultural "Jewfro" worn by Abbie Hoffman and Bob Dylan. People who have forgotten Angela Davis's political agenda remember her Afro, that humongous circle of reddish-brown hair.

The Afro traveled beyond America, migrating along the cultural routes of the Black Atlantic. Black debutantes in South Africa's segregated townships wore Afros. The Brazilian race pride movement, Black Rio, used the style. Contemporary black British artist Chris Ofili's psychedelic paintings of Afro-wearing women mark its inroads in black Europe. The Afro also resonated with 1960s design. According to Cara Greenberg, "the single most characteristic shape of the 1960s" was "the sphere" (1999:22). Several kinds of Afros flourished—close-cropped, a medium upsweep, the bushy—but they mostly imitated the sphere. Achieving a precise, rounded globe was the highest aesthetic goal. A radiant Leontyne Price appeared on the cover of *Opera News* in a perfectly spherical hairstyle. Roberta Flack's *Quiet Fire* album cover showed her with a similar orb. In design concept, the Afro belonged alongside Charles and Ray Eames's dome for the IBM Pavilion at the 1964 World's Fair.

The Afro crossed and played with boundaries, but its real power was in its disclosures. Carolyn Rodgers, writing in *Negro Digest* in 1967, saw wearing the Afro as a necessary collective psychological rite of passage, undoing the concealment, the deception, of straightened hair. "Who should wear the natural look?" she asked. Her answer: "All those who want to be black, beautiful and true" (1967:23). It was the truth-telling hairstyle.

Perhaps the Afro told too much truth. Quiet as this is kept, many blacks initially resisted conversion to the Afro. In 1963, the *Pittsburgh Courier* reported that a very successful traveling fashion revue with "fuzzy, au naturelle coiffure" models all wearing African dress, led by cultural-pace-setter and song stylist Abbey Lincoln, had also caused much dissension (1963:9). Even at the end of the Afro's reign there were still holdouts. James McPherson's story "The Faithful," in which an older black barber refuses to service Afro-wearers, is a snapshot from this counter-movement (1977). The Afro's triumph was neither sudden nor a seamless narrative.

Also complicating the Afro's story is the mistaken notion that it was spawned exclusively from the revolutionary ideas of the 1960s. As early as 1922, writing on "Some Things Negroes Need to Do," the historian Carter G. Woodson was arguing, "We must cease trying to straighten our hair and bleach our faces, and be Negroes— and be good ones" (see Aptheker 1990:349). He was not alone. Next to the ads for hair-straightening salons, New York's *Amsterdam News* of the 1920s and 1930s carried many opinions like those of the letter-writer E. T. Campbell, who chided those "aping the white man to the extent of straightening . . . kinky hair."

The Afro had an uneasy relationship with African hairstyles. East and southern Africa had styles broadly resembling the Afro, mostly of the close-cropped variety. Western African male styles looked like moderate Afros, and children wore similar styles. But an indigenous African Afro of the large variety did not exist. For this reason some African intellectuals worried about the hairstyle's arrival in Africa. It was criticized in Lagos, Nigeria (Darnton 1977:22). In Tanzania, Kadji Konde disparaged the style as "a cultural, imperialistic invasion." Konde went on to claim that the Afro "gnawed at the roots of the African personality" (*Jet* 1970:47). In Mali, on the other hand, according to Manthia Diawara, the youth of the city of Bamako adopted the Afro to stress their with-it cosmopolitanism (1998:99–108).

Ultimately the Afro put a klieg light on black hair. It was an epoch-making event. When tall and precisely shaped, and held high by a regal head tilt, the Afro was truly captivating—it was black hair in all its unpomaded, decolonized glory.

The Second Visibility: 1970s–1990s Hair Events:

As early as 1972, *Sepia* magazine asked "Is the Afro Over?" *Jet* magazine began running more photos of braid-wearers.[1] Cicely Tyson astonished television viewers with her Nigerian braided style—a dome of tiny arches. Newspapers raced her photo into print. Jettisoning her trademark Afro, Roberta Flack performed wearing an exuberant Zairian style, a cap of braids with a center geyser of hair.

The Afro moment was being challenged. In fact the Afro itself was being pared down, like the one worn by singer Kim Weston. A new era of black hairstyling and visibility was opening. In terms of hair, the era from the 1970s to the 1990s can be characterized as open-ended, exploratory, and diverse in styles. It was a time when many playful and fantasy styles flourished. Despite occasional political flare-ups, individual choice would increasingly dictate African-American hairstyles in this era. Jheri curls— a retro look of pomaded tresses, reminiscent of the styles of 1950s religious leaders Daddy Grace and Prophet Jones—was proof that 1960s orthodoxy had lost its grip. Black hair was still cultural politics, though, as *l'affaire* Bo Derek proved in 1980:

black entertainers criticized actress Derek for wearing cornrow braids in the movie *10* and suggesting she had invented the style.

Although this is rarely commented on, research played a crucial role as the period started up. A small cohort of black hair-culture connoisseurs began investigating the heritage of black hairstyles. Hungering for accurate information, they studied books on African art, texts on the Afro-Caribbean, museum exhibits, vintage photos, and specific African ethnic braiding traditions (Maasai braiding, for example). Young stylists were taught old African-American styles. The celebrated Malikia of Oakland, California—Stevie Wonder's braider—both studied African-American styles and visited Africa for instruction. Always ahead of her time, art historian Sylvia Ardyn Boone did fieldwork in Liberia on local hairstyles. Shedding insularity, these hair experts educated themselves about the immense hairstyle resources of black America and of the black diaspora.

Cornrows were the first of the heirloom styles to be widely revived. Braider Tulani Jordan has compared them to "corn crop rows . . . freshly planted food crops" (1983:65). Similar Caribbean braids were "canerows," after sugarcane rows. Cornrow hairstyling harked back to at least the eighteenth-century Americas.

Beginning in the 1970s, new West African emigrants from Liberia, Ghana, Nigeria, Sierra Leone, and Senegal brought their hairstyles into America's cities. One specific technique of theirs consisted of weaving or threading materials such as hair additions, colored string, dyed bark, shells, coins, buttons, and beads into a hairstyle. (Tennis stars Serena and Venus Williams owe West Africa!) A popular current technique—using extensions in braiding—would evolve from this. Storefront salons often disseminated these styles. In the 1980s, one such Harlem shop advertised "An African Braid Explosion":

Corkscrew	*Senegalese*	*TwistBoofruito*
Flat Twist	*Casamance*	*Spaghetti Braids*
Corn Rows	*Box Braids*	*African-American Plaits*
	Dubie Braids	

As this menu shows, braiding traditions—the African-American and the African—were cross-fertilizing each other. Dreadlocks, arrriving from their Rastafarian niche in Jamaica, added another option to the African-American hair repertoire, and brought a religious-mystical sense to black hair conceptions. The hair formations of Rastafari "had . . . early cultural roots among different tribes on the Afrikan Continent . . . the history of the Ihibhlhe (Bible/Scriptures) reveals that one of the covenants of the Nazarite was the adorning of locks" (Faristzaddi 1991:n.p.). Now black hair had scriptural sanction, to be revered as part of the divine human.

All these styles converging in black America set off a black hair "Big Bang" event, one that unleashed hair innovations *and* discourses about hair—a ferment still alive. It had not been easy: in 1977, cornrows almost got a U.S. Army woman court-martialed. Braids in the workplace prompted firings. In 1988, one such case became a major complaint before the federal Equal Employment Opportunity Commission. Wearers of dreadlocks were harassed by police. In the nation's capital, a braiding salon called Cornrows & Co. ran afoul of the Cosmetology Board, which alleged violations of licensing standards.

Still, acclaim awaited braiders. They would eventually be praised as "artists," their works called "creations," their body-healing manifestoes taken seriously. The rich and famous wanted their nimble fingers. Salons like New York's Khamit Kinks, or Atlanta's Braids Weaves and Things, became centers of a renaissance. Newspapers ran braid photo spreads, and dreadlocks got press too. A dreadlocked Lenny Kravitz graced a cover of the style magazine *Details*. On a cold 1990 February day, a braiding workshop was held at the Library of Congress; the event was swamped. Around the same time, a children's video called *Dreadlocks and the Three Bears* got unexpected praise.

From the mid-1980s on, the "fade" style emerged, mostly among men. At first it was just types of hair tapering. Later it added designs, lightly etched into the hair. These designs could be basic, like stripes or curves, or fanciful, like roses, a Mercedes emblem, basketball players, and on occasion pornography. The rap artist King Sun once wore a champagne glass complete with the word "Moet" and bubbles. At a young woman's funeral in San Francisco, her male friends wore her name in their hair. The media loved these designs, and when the shaved-head style spread among black men, they followed that too.

Whereas the Afro era was premised on hair conformity, the 1970s–'90s endorsed openness—a kind of *glasnost*, this time applied to hair. Lest we forget, however, there was a time when such freedom for black hair was rare—when African-Americans struggled for hair expressivity.

The Struggle for Hair Expressivity: From Africa to the 1950s

In an account of travel in western Africa written in 1602, the Dutchman Pieter de Marees was compelled to comment on hair. On men's styles he wrote, "They are very proud of the way in which they cut their hair, each in his own fashion and competing in style." Of one style for women he reported, "Their head is well dressed, their hair being frizzled and plaited to a point"; of another, "they also use . . . beads . . . which they hang and plait in their hair." And he observed of the women of Benin, "They shave [cut] their hair in various ways, each after the finest manner and fashion possible" (1987:39, 171, 174, 231).

From the reports of Marees and others, it is clear that western Africa had an expressive hair culture early on. Braiding, decorated hair, many haircuts for men, shaving, hair extensions, women wearing men's styles, the use of combs, spikes—all these were present. Hairstyles could communicate status, occupation, group affiliation. In affluent towns where intense social promenading took place, hairstyling was as changing and rivalry-driven as in London or Amsterdam: "Among fifty men one would not find two or three with the same haircut" (ibid.:33). In these bustling communities, hairstyles had to be deft and bold.

In America during the seventeenth and eighteenth centuries, as thousands of Africans were imported to be slaves, parts of this proud hair culture survived, often through reinvention. Braiding reappeared in America. Head shaving was brought over as a male style, reinforced by similar Native American styles; long hair too was

Fig. 122. "Locks Heaven," Brooklyn, 1987.
Photo: Chester Higgins, Jr.

reported among both men and women. A watercolor of 1797 by Henry Latrobe shows male slaves with plaits down the back of their heads, a hybrid of African and European hair fashion. Exhibiting an African taste for hair novelty and comment, some men shaped their hair to mimic high-status wigs.

The real suppression of black hair-expressivity began in the nineteenth century. A tougher form of slavery, and a dwindling in the numbers of incoming Africans, caused a narrowing and simplifying of styles. Shorter hair for men and women prevailed. Women's hair gradually came to be concealed by a head wrap or bandanna. Sunday was the only time slaves could display their most artful hair, and was the day women donned their finest bandannas. Keeping hair healthy was also an everyday struggle.

Black hair itself came in for attack. Abusing the hair of slaves by disfiguring it was a favorite punishment. Masters' jealous wives cut off the hair of slave women. It was common to mock slaves' "kinky hair." By the 1850s, Peter A. Browne, a self-proclaimed scientist, was contending that "the Negro has on his head wool and not hair," and that "since the white man has hair, they belong to two distinct species" (1850:20). When slavery ended, in 1865, the parodying of black hair intensified. Minstrel shows spread. Representations of "pickaninny" hair as ugly appeared in ads and on products.

Where did African-American hairstyling go in this pernicious climate? It is often assumed that after slavery, straightening became the goal. The greasing or "larding" of hair had emerged during slavery; combined with primitive hair-pressing later on, this became the basic model of hair straightening. Yet studio photographs from the 1880s–1900s show that many pretty, clever natural styles were then in play. There was no stampede to straightening, which only achieved hegemony in the 1910s–'20s.

It is also too simple to argue that it was admiration of whites, and of their hair, that explains the success of hair straightening. Other factors counted. Ambitious female self-improvers and racial-uplifters, a professional class in the making, wanted a new look. Black beauty tracts projected a different future aesthetic. Rural blacks migrating to cities, particularly men, imagined waved hair as encoding their new urbanity. Even in the rural areas of black America, slight hairstyle changes could be seen: a few photographs showing styles from North Carolina barbershops of the 1930s reveal men getting cuts that allowed more hair and have sharp, almost geometrical edges.

Into this fertile situation stepped Sarah Breedlove (1867–1919), who entered the hair business as an agent for Annie Turnbo Malone, the St. Louis manufacturer of Wonderful Hair Grower shampoo. After developing a product line of her own, Breedlove married Charles J. Walker (a helpful advertising and mail-order expert), moved her business to Indianapolis, and renamed herself "Madam" C. J. Walker, hinting at links to Parisian coiffure. Indeed her career resembles that of the revolutionary French hair innovator Marcel Grateau (1852–1936), the inventor of the wavy marcel hairstyle, which made him an exceptionally rich man. Walker would become one of the great beauty-culture business people of the twentieth century. A one-person hair event, she invented products, adapted the straightening iron for black hair, promoted door-to-door sales, trained women beauticians, opened salons, and franchised her services. She was easily the equal of Helena Rubenstein and Elizabeth Arden. Just as important, she prepared the way for many new straightened styles, which were alluring in their time, and inspired a new hair expressivity.

Walker repeatedly denied that she merely straightened hair. Instead, she wanted "the great mass of [her] people to take greater pride in their personal appearance and give their hair proper attention" (Rooks 1996:63). She creatively recast the issue of straightening into concerns about health, achievement, and beauty. After World War II, however, just when straightening seemed most entrenched, its years were actually numbered. Most devastating to the practice was a critique hammered home by Malcolm X and others: for blacks to erase their natural features was a reflection of self-hatred. To accuse Walker of subverting the natural qualities of the black body, however, is to overlook the possibility, recently argued by Kobena Mercer, that straightening hair played off white hair, was a cultural riff on it—or a third way *between* black and white hair, a creole phenomenon (1994:114–23). By this logic, black men's conks—a 1950s straightened style—did not copy white men's hair.

In any case, when the Afro came on the scene, it unseated straightening and revalorized the black hair—that wool!—attacked so viciously in the nineteenth century.

Future Black Hair Events

African-Americans today wear a greater diversity of hair textures, lengths, styles, and combo styles than ever before. Everything seems in! The hair magazine *Color and Cut* even urges, "Dare to be wrong and be different" (1999:39). Black hair is at the apex of its public presence. It is seen in more variety, and is more widely discussed, than ever before.

Beyond this, two future hair events or trends are emerging. First, interest in black hair is surging among black artists. Notable figures who have embraced the subject include Sonia Boyce, Robert Colescott, David Hammons, Barkley Hendricks, Chris Ofili, Sandra Payne, Adrian Piper, Alison Saar, Lorna Simpson, and Carrie Mae Weems, to name a few. What drives these artists is the probing of the intersection between everyday, quotidian black hair and hypercharged, racialized black hair. As we have seen, this is the key intersection for black hair's history in America. In all likelihood this artistic surge—because of its conceptual richness—will continue.

A second trend exists that might be called "hair morphing." The old idea that black hair and white hair are homogenous polar opposites is crumbling. In recent months, cultural commentators as different as *New York Times* columnist Margo Jefferson and comic Chris Rock are gleefully questioning this idea. Most subversive of it, however, are the hairstyles themselves. Contemporary African-American styles often incorporate elements that disregard ethnic definitions. The most obvious example is the rage for blonde, true red, or red-orange coloring for black hair. Simultaneously with this, other Americans are gradually deriving pleasure from so-called black styles, particularly braiding. Look at new magazines and books illustrating hair—the African-American magazine *Passion* or the Euro-American-oriented book *The Mane Thing* (Mancuso 1999)—and see if black hair and white hair can be separated. They cannot. Instead, they are subtly morphing and transforming into each other.

Still, there are sure to be surprise black hair events, especially as long as people like risk-taking Latrell Sprewell and his merry ad-makers are around. Stay tuned!

1. See for example the issues of June 17, 1971, pp. 36–37; December 28, 1972, p. 33; May 9, 1974, p. 36; and July 11, 1974, p. 14.

Bibliography

Abimbola, Wande. "The Yoruba Concept of Human Personality," in *La Notion de Personne en Afrique Noire*. Paris: Colloques Internationaux du Centre National de la Recherche Scientifique, no. 544, 1971.
———. *Ifa: An Exposition of Ifa Literary Corpus*. Ibadan, Nigeria: Oxford University Press, 1976.
———. "The Place of African Traditional Religion in Contemporary Africa: The Yoruba Example," in *African Traditional Religion in Contemporary Society* edited by Jacob K. Olupona. New York: Paragon House, 1991, pp. 51-58.

Abiodun, Rowland. "A Reconsideration of the Function of Ako, Second Burial Effigy in Owo," in *Africa*, vol. 46, no.1, 1976, pp. 4–20.
———. "Verbal and Visual Metaphors: Mythical Allusions in Yoruba Ritualistic Art of Ori," in *Ife: Annals of the Institute of African Studies*, no. 1, 1986, pp. 8–39.
———. "The Kingdom of Owo," in *Yoruba: Nine Centuries of African Art and Thought*. New York: The Center for African Art and Harry N. Abrams Publishers Inc., 1989, pp. 91–115.

Adeoye, C. Laogun. *Asa ati Ise Yoruba*. Oxford: Oxford University Press, 1979.
———. *Igbagbo ati Esin Yoruba*. Ibadan, Nigeria: Evans Brothers, 1989.

Afrika Museum. *Haar in De Hoofdrol*. Berg en Dal: Afrika Museum, 1986.

"Afro Hairdo Upsets African Writer," in *Jet*, November 26, 1970.

Ajanaku, Fagbemi. "Ori, Ipin ati Kadara, Apoa Keji," in *Olokun*, no. 10, 1972, pp. 11–13.

Ajibola, J. O. *Owe Yoruba*. Ibadan, Nigeria: African University Press Ltd., 1978.

Akinnuoye, Susan F. *Nigerian Hair Styles*. Ibadan, Nigeria: Sketch Publishing Company, n.d.

Alade, M. "Ori, Ipin ati Kadara, Apa Kini," in *Olokun* no. 10, 1972, pp. 8–10.

Alldridge, Thomas J. *The Sherbro and Its Hinterland*. London: Macmillan and Co., 1901.

Anonymous. *Reisgids Belgisch Congo en Ruanda Urundi*. Brussels: Infor Congo en Dienst voor voorlichting en publieke relaties van Belgisch Congo, Dienst Toerisme (1 ste uitgave), 1949.

Apter, Andrew. *Black Critics and Kings: The Hermeneutics of Power in Yoruba Society*. Chicago: University of Chicago Press, 1992.

Aptheker, Herbert, ed. *A Documentary History of the Negro People in the United States*, vol. 3. New York: Citadel Press, 1990.

Araba, Oloye Ajanaku. "Ero ati Igbagbo Awon Yoruba Nipa Olorun", in *Iwe Asa Ibile Yoruba* edited by Oludare Olajubu. Lagos, Nigeria: Longman, 1978, pp. 1–11.

Arnoldi, Mary Jo and Christine Kreamer Mueller. *Crowning Achievements: African Arts of Dressing the Head*. Los Angeles: University of California, Los Angeles, Fowler Museum of Cultural History, 1995.

"Arts of Black Africa," in *Sabena Revue*, no. 1, 1974, pp. 1-96.
Astley, Thomas. *A New General Collection of Voyages and Travel. Vols. I–IV, 1745*. London: Frank Cass and Company Limited, 1968.

Atkins, John. *A Voyage to Guine*. London: Ward and Chandler, 1737.

"'Au Naturelle' Revue Sparks Controversy," in *Pittsburgh Courier*. March 9, 1963.

Babayemi, Solomon. "Oyo Palace Organization: Past and Present" in *African Notes*, vol. 10, no. 1, 1986, pp. 4–24.

Baduel, C. and C. Meillassoux. "Modes et codes de la coiffure Ouest-Africaine," in *Société d'Ethnographie de Paris*, no. 69, 1, 1975, pp. 11–59.

Bascom, William. *The Yoruba of Southwestern Nigeria*. New York: Holt Rhinehart and Winston, 1969.

Bastin, Marie-Louise. *Art décoratif Tshokwe*. Dundo:Diamang, 1961.
———. *La Sculpture tshokwe*. Meudon: Alain et Françoise Chaffin, 1982.
———. *Escultura Angolana: memorial de culturas*. Lisbon: Museu Nacional de Etnologia, 1995.

Becker, R. *Tsonga Headrests: The Making of an Art History Category*. PhD. Thesis. Johannesburg: University of the Witwaterstand, 1999.
———. "South Africa," in *Africa: The Art of a Continent,* edited by T. Phillips. Munich, New York: Prestel, 1995.

Beier, Ulli. "Signwriters' Art in Nigeria" in *African Arts*, vol. IV, no. 3, Spring 1971, pp.22-27.

Bernatzik, Hugo Adolf. *Zwischen Weissen Nile und Belgisch Kongo*. Wien: Lwseidel und Son, 1929.
———. *Der Dunkle Erditeil: Afrika*. Berlin: Atlantis Verlag, 1930.
———. *Athiopen des Westens: Forschungsreisen in Portugiesisch Guinea. 2 Vols*. Wien: Lwseidel und Son, 1933.

Bernolles, J. *Permanence de la parure et du masque africains*. Paris: G. P. Maisonneuve et Larose, 1966.

Biebuyck, Daniel and N. Van Den Abbeele. *The Power of the Headdresses, A Cross-cultural Study of Forms and Functions*. Brussels: Tendi S.A., 1984.

Boone, Sylvia Arden. *Radiance from the Waters*. New haven: Yale University Press, 1986.

Bourgeois, Arthur. "Yaka and Suku Leadership Headgear," in *African Arts* vol. XV, no. 3, 1982, pp. 30-35, 92.

Brier, Bob. *The Encyclopedia of Mummies*. New York: Checkmark Books, 1998.

Bryant, A. T. *The Zulu People*. Pietermaritzburg: Shuter & Shooter, 1949.

Burssens, H. *Mangbetu: Afrikaanse hofkunst uit Belgische prive-verzamelingen*. Brussels: Kredietbank, 1992.

Browne, Peter A. *Classification of Mankind, by the Hair and Wool of Their Heads*. Philadelphia: A. Hart, 1850.

Büttikofer, Johann. *Reisebilder Aus Liberia, 2 Vols*. Leiden: E. J. Brill. 1890.

Cameron, Elisabeth. "Negotiating Gender:Initiation Arts of Mwadi and Mukanda Among the Lunda and Luvale Kabomp District, North-Western Province, Zambia." Unpublished Dissertation, Los Angeles: UCLA.
———. *Isn't S/He a Doll? Play Ritual in African Sculpture*. Los Angeles: UCLA Fowler Museum of Cultural History, 1996.

Cameron, Verney Lovett. *Across Africa*. New York: Harper and Brothers, 1877.

Capart, D. "L'origine africaine des coiffures egyptiennes," in *Reflet du mode,* no. 8, February, 1956, pp. 3-26.

Capello, H. R. Ivens. *De Benguella as terras de Iacca.* Lisboa: Imprensa Nacional, 1881.

Cardinall, A.W. *In Ashanti and Beyond.* Philadelphia: J. B. Lippincott Company, 1927.

Cardoso, A. da Fonseca. *Em terras do Moxico.* Porto: Sociedade Portuguesa de Antropolgia e Etnologia, 1903.

Carvalho, H. A. Dias de. *Ethnographie e historia tradicional dos povos de Lunda.* Lisboa: Imprensa Nacional, 1890.

Casati, G. *Dix annees en Equatoria. Le retour d'Emin Pacha et l'expedition Stanley. Traduit par Louis de Hessem.* Paris: Firmin Didot &C., 1892.

Cole, Herbert M. "Vital Arts in Northern Kenya," in *African Arts,* vol. VII, no. 2, Winter 1974, pp.12-23, 78.

Cole, Herbert and Doran H. Ross. *The Arts of Ghana.* Los Angeles: Museum of Cultural History University of California, 1977.

Cordwell, Justine M. "Naturalism and Stylization in Yoruba Art," in *Magazine of Art,* vol.46, 1953, pp. 220–225.

The Cudahy-Massee-Milwaukee Museum African Expedition, 1928-29. Westport: Greenwood Press, Publishers, reprint ed. 1970.

Cut and Color: Sensationnel, vol. 1. New York: 32ⁿᵈ Avenue Corporation, 1999.

Czekanowski, J. *Wissenschaftliche ergebnisse der Deutschen Zentral_Afrika Expedition (1907-1908) unter fuhrung A. Friedrichs, Herzogs zu Mecklengurg. Band VI 2. Ethnographie?Antropologie.* Leipzig: Klinkhardt & Biermann, 1924.
———. *Forschungen im Nil_Kongo-Zwischengebiet. Band V. Azande, Uele-Stamme, Niloten.* Leipzig: Klinkhardt & Biermann, 1927.

Dapper, Olfert. *Naukeurige beschrijvinge der Afriaensche gewestern.* Amsterdam: Jacob van Meurs, 1668.

Daramola, Olu, and A. Jeje. *Awon Asa ati Orisa Ile Yoruba.* Ibadan, Nigeria: Onibonoje Press and Book Industries, 1975.

Darnton, Nina. "Lagos Hairstyles Reflect African History (and the Afro is a Put-On Wig)," in *New York Times,* January 6, 1977.

Daye, Pierre, Jacques Crokaert, J.-M. Jadot, A. Gilson, Pierre Ryckmans, L. Guebels, Paul Fontainas, Paul Salkin, Philippe Soupault, Dr. J. Maës, H. Schouteden. *Le Miroir du Congo Belge, Vols. I & II.* Bruxelles, Paris: Aux Editions, Nationale d'Éditions Artistiques, 1929.

Diawara, Manthia. *In Search of Africa.* Cambridge: Harvard University Press, 1998.

Dingwall, J. *Artificial Cranial Deformation.* London, 1931.

Dopamu, P.A. "Yoruba Magic and Medicine and their Relevance for Today" in *Journal of the Nigerian Association of Religious Studies,* vol. 4, 1979, pp. 3–20.

Dos Santos, Juana E. and Descoredes Dos Santos. "Esu Bara: Principle of Individual Life in the Nago System" in *La Notion de Personne en Afrique Noire.* Paris: Colloques Internationaux du Center National de la Recherche Scientifique, no. 544, 1971.

Douglas, M. *Purity and Danger: An Analysis of the Concepts of Pollution and Taboo.* London: Routledge and Kegan, 1966.

Drewal, Henry J. and John Mason. *Beads, Body, and Soul: Art, Light in the Yoruba Universe.* Los Angeles: UCLA Fowler Museum of Cultural History, 1998.

Drewal, Henry J., John Pemberton, and Rowland Abiodun. *Yoruba: Nine Centuries of African Art and Thought.* New York: The Center for African Art and Harry N. Abrams Publishers Inc., 1989.

Drewal, Margaret T. *Yoruba Ritual: Performers, Play, Agency.* Bloomington: Indiana University Press, 1992.

Driberg, J. H. "Note on Hairdressing among the Lango," in *Man,* 37/38, 1919.

Ellis, A. B. *The Tshi-Speaking Peoples of the Gold Coast of West Africa Their Religion, Manners, Customs, Laws, Language, etc.* The Netherlands: Anthropological Publications of Oosterhout N. B., 1887, reprint ed. 1966.

Estermann, Carlos. *Album de Penteados do Sudoeste de Angola.* Lisboa: Imprensa Portuguesa, 1960.
———. *Etnografia de Angola.* Vol. I, II. Lisboa: Instituto de Investigacal Cientifica Tropical, 1983.

Euba, Titi. "The Ooni of Ife's Are Crown and the Concept of Divine Head," in *Nigeria Magazine,* vol. 53, no.1, 1985, pp. 1–18.

Fajana, A. "Some Aspects of Yoruba Traditonal Education," in *Odu, University of Ife Journal of African Studies,* vol. 3, no. 1, 1996, pp. 16–28.

Felix, Marc and Manuel Jordán. *Makishi Lva Zambia: Mask Characters of the Upper Zambezi Peoples.* Munich: Fred Jahn, 1998.

Fischer, Eberhard, Hans Himmelheber. *Die Kunst der Dan.* Zurich: Museum Rielberg, 1976.

Franck, Louis, Minister van Staat. *Belgisch Congo.* Antwerp: De Sikkel, 1930.

Freeman, Richard Austin. *Travels and Life in Ashanti and Jaman.* New York: Frederick A. Stokes Company, 1898.

Frehn, B., T. Krings. *Afrikanische Frisuren. Symbolik und Formenvielfait traditioneller und moderner Haartrachten im westafrikanischen Sahel und Sudan.* Cologne: DuMont Buchverlag, 1986.

Giovenditto, A. "La deformazione artificiale della testa e la sua diffusione nella zona africana," in *Nigrizia* no.1, 1958, p. 17.

Greenberg, Cara. *From Op to Pop: Furniture of the 1960s.* Boston, New York, and London: Bulfinch Press, 1999.
———. *Itations of Jamaica and Irastafari.* Miami, 1991.

Guerinelle, N. "Note sur la place du corps dans les cultures africaines," in *Journal des Africanistes,* T.L., fasc., no. 2, 1980, pp.113-129.

Hair, P.E.H. (General editor) *Barbot on Guinea The Writings of Jean Barbot on West Africa 1678-1712.* Vols. I & II. London: The Hakluyt Society, 1992.

Hallpike, Christopher R. "Social Hair," in *Man,* vol. 4, 1969, pp. 256-264.

Hambly, Wilfrid D. *The Ovimbundu of Angola.* Chicago:Field Museum of Natural History, 1934.

Hamilton, C. "Women and Material Markers of Identity" in *Evocations of the Child,* edited by Dell. Johannesburg: Johannesburg Art Gallery and Human and Rousseua, 1998.

Himmelheber, Hans und Ulrike. *Die Dan ein Bauernvolk im Westafrikanischen Urwald.* Stuttgart: Verlag W. Kohlhammer GmbH., 1958.

Houlberg, Marilyn, ed. *Social Hair: Tradition and Change in Yoruba Hairstyles in Southwestern Nigeria*. Lagos: Craft Centre, National Museum, 1971.

Houlberg, Marilyn. "Social Hair: Yoruba Hairstyles in Southwestern Nigeria," in *Fabrics of Culture: The Anthropology of Clothing and Adornment,* edited by Justine M. Cordwell and Ronald A. Schwarz, The Hague: Mouton Publishers, 1979, pp. 349–397.

Hutchinson, Margarite. *A Report of the Kingdom of Congo and of the Surrounding Countries*. New York: Negro Universities Press, 1969.

Hutchinson, Walter, ed. *Customs of the World, A Popular Account of the Manners, Rites and Ceremonies of Men and Women in All Countries, vols. I and II*. London: Hutchinson & Co., 1913.

Hutereau, A. *1911-1913 Fieldnotes*. Archives. Tervuren: Ethnography Division, Royal Museum for Central Africa.
———. *Histoire des peuplades de L'Uele et de l'Ubangi*. Brussels: Goemaere, 1921.

Idowu, E. Bolaji. *Olodumare: God in Yoruba Belief*. New York: Original Publications, 1995.

John Michael Kohler Arts Center. *Hair*. Wisconsin: John Michael Kohler Arts Center, 1993.

Johnson, Samuel. *The History of the Yorubas*. Lagos, Nigeria: CMS Bookshops, 1921.
———. *The History of the Yoruba From the Earliest Times to the Beginning of the British Protectorate*. Lagos: CMS (Nigeria) Bookshop Lagos, 1957.

Jordán, Manuel. "Tossing Life in a Basket: Art and Divination Among Chokwe, Lunda, Luvale and Related Peoples of Northwestern Zambia." The University of Iowa, Unpublished Dissertation, 1996.

Jordan, Tulani L. C. "The History and Significance of Hair Braiding," in *The Black Collegian*, April/May 1983.

Junod, Blaise. *Bantu Heritage*. Johannesburg: Hortors Limited, 1958.

Junker, W. *Travels in Africa during the Years 1875-1878*. Trans A. H. Keane. London: Chapman and Hall, 1870.

Klopper, Sandra. *The Art of Zulu-speakers in Northern Natal-Zululand: an Investigation of the History of Beadwork, Carving, and Dress from Shaka to Inkatha*. PhD. Thesis University of the Witwatersrand, Johannesburg, 1992.

———. "Chapter 3: South Africa," In Phillips, T. (ed) *Africa: the Art of a Continent*. Munich and New York: Prestel, 1995, pp.207-208.

Koné, Mamadou. *Coiffures Traditionnelles et Modernes au Mali*. Bamako: Editions Populaires, 197-.

Kouavovi, B. M. "La coiffure chez les Noirs de l'Afrique occidentale et ses rapports avec l'art, l'occultisme et la medicine," in *Encyclopedie mensuelle d'outre-mer,* vol. 5, no. 59, July 1955, pp.334-336.

Ladele, T. A. A. *Akojopo Iwadi Ijinle Asa Yoruba*. Lagos, Nigeria: Macmillan Nigeria Publishers, Ltd., 1986.

Lang, H. *1909-1914 Fieldnotes*. *Archives. Department of Anthropology*. New York: American Museum of Natural History.

Lawal, Babatunde. "Some Aspects of Yoruba Aesthetics," in *The British Journal of Aesthetics*, vol. 15, no. 3, 1974, pp. 239–249.
———."The Living Dead: Art and Immortality Among the Yoruba of Nigeria," in *Africa*, vol. 47, no. 1, 1977, pp. 50–61.
———. "Ori: The Significance of the Head in Yoruba Sculpture," in *The Journal of Anthropological Research*, vol. 41, no. 1, 1985, pp. 91–103.
———. "A Ya gbo, A Ya To: New Perspective on Edan Ogboni," in *African Arts*, vol. 28, no. 1, 1995, pp. 36–49, 98–100.
———. *The Gelede Spectacle: Art, Gender, and Social Harmony in an African Culture*. Seattle and London: University of Washington Press, 1996.

Leach, Edmond R. "Magic Hair," in *Journal of Research Anthropological Research Inst.* 88, 1956, pp. 147-164.

Lelong, M. H., o.p. *Mes freres du Congo. 2 vols.* Alger: Editions Baconnier, 1946.

Maes, J. "Déformation cranienne chez les Mangbetu du Congo Belge," in *Le Progres* , no. 11, May 1936, pp. 26–29.

Mancuso, Kevin. *The Mane Thing*. New York: Little, Brown and Company, 1999.

de Marees, Pieter. *Description and Historical Account of the Gold Kingdom of Guinea*. 1602. Reprint ed. Oxford: at the University Press, 1987.

McLeod, M.D. *The Asante*. London: British Museum Publications Ltd., 1981.

McPherson, James. "The Faithful," in *Elbow Room*. Boston: Little, Brown and Company, 1977.

Mercer, Kobena. *Welcome to the Jungle: New Positions in Black Cultural Studies*. New York: Routledge, 1994.

Mostert, N. *Frontiers: The Epic of South Africa's Creation and the Tragedy of the Xhosa People*. London: Pimlico, 1992.

Mustapha, Oyebamiji, Dele Ajayi, and Adebisi Amoo. *Osupa Ede Yoruba*, vol. 2. Lagos, Nigeria: Nelson Publishers Ltd., 1986.

de Negri, E. *Nigerian Body Adornments*. Lagos: Academic Press, 1976.

Nel, K. "Chapter 3: Southern Africa," in. *Africa: The Art of a Continent* edited by Tom Phillips. Munich and New York: Prestel. 1995.

Nettleton, A. "Chapter 3: Southern Africa," in *Africa: The Art of a Continent* edited by Tom Phillips. Munich and New York: Prestel, 1995.

Nooter, Mary H. *Secrecy: African Art that Conceals and Reveals*. New York and Munich: The Museum of African Art and Prestel, 1993.

Ogunwale, Titus A. "Traditional Hairdressing in Nigeria," in *African Arts*, vol. V, no. 3, Spring 1972, pp.44-45.

Ojo, G. J. Afolabi and G. J. Afolabi. *Yoruba Culture: A Geographic Analysis*. London and Nigeria: University of Ife and University of London Press, 1966.

Okemuyiwa, Gbolahan, and Ademola Fabunmi. "Ori," in *Orunmila* no. 4, 1989, pp. 15–20.

Olaniyan, Richard. "Elements of Yoruba Traditional Diplomacy: An Assessment," in *Yoruba Oral Traditon,* edited by Wande Abimbola, Ile-Ife, Nigeria, 1975, pp. 293–332.

Paulme, D. and Brosse, J. *Parures africaines*. Paris: Hachette, 1956.

Pearson, Emil. *People of the Aurora*. San Diego: Beta Books, 1977.

Pemberton, John. "Eshu-Elegba: The Yoruba Trickster God," in *African Arts*, vol. 9, no. 1, 1975, pp. 20–27, 66–70, 90–91.

Phillips, Ruth B. "The Iconography of the Mende Sowei Mask" in *Ethnologische Zeitschrift Zurich,* no. 1, 1980, pp. 113-132.

Phillips, Tom, ed. *Africa: The Art of a Continent*. Munich and New York: Prestel, 1995.

Picton, John. "Art, Identity, and Identification," in *The Yoruba Artist: New Theoretical Perspectives on African Arts*, edited by Rowland Abiodun, Henry J. Drewal, and John Pemberton. Washington and London: Smithsonian Institution Press, 1994.

Pigafetta, Filippo. *A Report of the Kingdom of Congo, and the Surrounding Countries; Drawn out of the Writings and Deicourses of the Portuguese, Duarte Lopez.* 1591. Translated by Margarite Hutchinson, 1881. Reprint ed. New York: Negro Universities Press, 1969.

Poynor, Robin. *Spirit's Eyes, Human Hands:African Art at the Harn Museum.* Gainesville: University Press of Florida, 1995.

Rachewiltz de, Boris. *Black Eros Sexual Customs of Africa From Prehistory to the Present Day.* New York: Lyle Stuart, Inc., 1964.

Rattray, Captain R. S. *Religion and Art in Ashanti.* Oxford: Clarendon Press, 1927.

Redinha, José. *Etnias e culturas de Angola.* Luanda: I.I.C.A. 1975.

Reynolds, Barrie. *The Material Culture of the Peoples of the Gwembe Valley.* Manchester: Manchester University Press for the National Museum of Zambia, 1968.

Roberts, Allen. *Animals in African Art: From the Familiar to the Marvelous.* New York and Munich: The Museum for African Art and Prestel, 1995.
———. "Les arts du corps chez les Tabwa," in *Art d'Afrique Noire*, 1986, pp. 15-29.

Roberts, Allen and Evan Maurer. *Tabwa: The Rising of a New Moon.* Seattle: University of Washington Press for the University Museum of Art, 1985.

Rodgers, Carolyn. "Truth *IS* Black Beauty," in *Negro Digest,* no. 17, 1967.

Rodrigues de Areia, Manuel L. *Les symboles divinatoires.* Portugal: Coimbra University, 1985.

Rooks, Noliwe M. *Hair Raising: Beauty, Culture, and African American Women.* New Brunswick: Rutgers University Press, 1996.

Sagay, E. *African Hairstyles: Styles of Yesterday and Today.* London: N.H. Exter, 1983.

Scherz, Anneliese, Ernst R. Scherz, G Taapopi, and A Otto. *Hair-styles, Head-dresses & Ornaments in Namibia &*

Southern Angola. Windhoek, Namibia: Gamsberg Macmillan Publishers (Pty) Ltd., 1981 (reprint ed. 1992).

Schildkrout, Enid and Curtis A. Keim (eds). *African Reflections: Art from Northeastern Zaire.* New York: American Museum of Natural History and University of Washington Press, 1990.

Schweeger-Hefel, A, and W. Staude. *Die Kurumba von Lurum, Monographie eines Volkes aus Obervolta (Westafrika).* Wien: Verlag A. Schendl, 1972.

Schmidt, Max. *The Primitive Races of Mankind, A Study in Ethnology.* Translated by Alexander K. Dallas. London: George G. Harrap & Co. Ltd., 1926.

Schweinfurth, George. *Au coeur de l'Afrique. Voyages et decouvertes dans les regions inexplorees de l'Afrique-central (1868-1871). 2 vols.* Traduit par H. Loreau. Paris: Hachette et Co., 1875.

The Secret Museum of Mankind, Five Volumes in One. New York: Manhattan House, n.d.

Seligman, C. and Seligman, B. Z. *Pagan Tribes of the Nilotic Sudan.* London: George Routledge and Sons, Ltd.,1932.

Shapiro, H. J. *A Correction for Artificial Deformation of Skulls.* Anthropological Papers of the American Museum of Natural History, XXX, I, 1928.

Shaw, E. M. and N. J. Van Warmelo. *The Material Culture of the Cape Nguni, Part 4: Personal and General, Annals of the South African Museum, Volume 58.* Cape Town: South African Museum, 1988.

Silverman, Raymond A. *History , Art and Assimilation, The Impact of Islam on Akan Material Culture.* Washington: University of Washington, 1983.

Sowande, Fela and Fagbemi Ajanaku. *Oruko Amutorunwa.* Ibadan, Nigeria: Oxford University Press, 1969.

Talbot, P. Amaury. *The Peoples of Southern Nigeria,* vol. 2, London: Oxford University Press, 1926.

Tayeye, Mayanga. *Coiffures du Zaire, series II,* vol. 53, 1979.

Thompson, Robert Farris. "The Sign of the Divine King: Yoruba Bead-Embroidered Crowns with Veil and Bird Decorations," in *African Art and Leadership,* edited by Douglas Fraser and Herbert M. Cole. Madison: University of Wisconsin Press. 1972, pp. 227–260.

Vandenhoute, P. J. *Classification Stylistique du Masque Dan et Guere de la Cote d'Ivoire Occidentale.* Leiden: E. J. Brill (Mededelingen van het Rijksmuseum voor Volkenkunde, Leiden nr. 4), 1948.
———. *Het Masker in de Cultuur en de Kunst van het Boven-Cavally-gebied. (Results of the Ivory Coast Expedition).* Doctoral dissertation manuscript, 1945.

Van Overbergh, C. and E. De Jonghe, E. *Les Mangbetu.* Brussels: Institut international de bibliographie, A. De Wit, 1909.

Vansina, Jan. *Art History of Africa.* London: Longsman, 1984.

Verger, Pierre. "The Yoruba High God-A Review of the Sources," in *Odu, University of Ife Journal of African Studies,* vol. 2, no.2, 1966, pp. 19–40.

Vogel, Susan. *Baule: African Art/Western Eyes.* New Haven: Yale University Press, 1997.

Warren, Dennis M. *The Akan of Ghana: an overview of the ethnographic literature.* Accra: Pointer Limited, 1973.

Waterman, Christopher. *Juju: A Social History and Ethnography of an African Popular Music.* Chicago: University of Chicago Press, 1990.

Weeks, John H. *Among the Primitive Bakongo,. A Record of Thirty Years' Close Intercourse with the Bakongo and other Tribes of Equatorial Africa, with a Description of Their Habits, Customs and Religious Beliefs.* New York: Negro Universities Press, 1969.

Wingert, Paul. "Style Determinants in African Sculpture," *in African Arts,* vol. V, no. 3, Spring 1972, pp.37-43.

Biographies of the essayists

Elze Bruyninx, who has been with the University of Ghent since 1970, wrote her doctoral dissertation on the brass art of the Dan and the Wè(Ivory Coast-Liberia). She has been head of the Department of Ethnic Art at her alma mater since 1991.

Els De Palmenaer studied Ethnic Art at the University of Ghent. From 1994 to 1999, she worked at the ethnographic department of the Royal Museum for Central Africa in Tervuren. She has co-edited the catalogue *Schatten uit het Afrika Museum (Tervuren)* [*Treasures from the Africa Museum (Tervuren)*], published in 1995. At present, she is responsible for the African collection at the Etnografisch Museum Antwerpen.

Frank Herreman, the Director of Exhibitions at the Museum for African Art since 1995, was formerly Associate Director of the Historical Museums of the City of Antwerp and a Professor of the Arts of Africa and Oceania at the Royal Academy of Fine Arts. He has curated numerous exhibitions of African and Oceanic art including the acclaimed *Face of the Spirits; Masks from the Zaire Basin*, 1994, which premiered in Belgium and traveled internationally. Mr. Herreman has lectured and published extensively on African art including an essay in the Royal Academy's major catalogue, *Africa: the Art of a Continent*.

Kennell Jackson is an Associate Professor of History at Stanford University, specializing in African History, particularly East African history. Recently, his interests have widened to include Black popular culture or mass culture. His most recent publication is *America Is Me*, a question-and-answer history of African-Americans that grew out of his directorship of Stanford's Afro-American studies program in the 1980s. He is curently working on a number of projects, one of which is a history of the Black body in the 20th century.

Manuel Jordán is Curator of the Arts of Africa and the Americas at the Birmingham Museum of Art. He is considered a foremost scholar of Chokwe art and culture, having lived among the Lunda, Luvale, Chokwe and related groups of northwestern Zambia for over two years, and visited Angolan museum collections. He has organized numerous exhibitions, among them, *CHOKWE! Art and Initiation Among Chokwe and Related Peoples*, and has published and lectured extensively on related subjects.

Babatunde Lawal, formerly Chairman, Department of Fine Arts and Dean, Faculty of Arts, University of Ife (now Obafemi Awolowo University), Nigeria, is Professor of Art History, Virginia Commonwealth University, and has served as Visiting Professor at many other institutions here and abroad. He has published extensively on traditional and contemporary African art, with particular expertise on Yoruba art and culture. He has a newly published book entitled, *The Gelede Spectacle: Art, Gender, and Social Harmony* and is working on another, *Sango Sculpture among the Yoruba of Nigeria.*

Niangi Batulukisi, born and educated in the Democratic Republic of the Congo, earned both a Master's Degree in African Studies and Ph.D. in Archaeology and Art History in Belgium, where she presently resides. Since 1982, she has served as an Assistant Professor in the Department of History at the University of Lubumbashi. She has published widely on Holo sculpture based on extensive field research among the Holo people of the Democratic Republic of Congo. She has also written on the Kongo peoples, sculpture of the Yaka and studies in the arts of Tanzania.

Karel Nel is an Associate Professor in the Department of Fine Arts at the University of the Witwatersrand, Johannesburg, South Africa. His particular interests have focused on sacred art which has led him to look closely at the value systems encoded in African, Oceanic and Eastern art. Southern African material is his particular expertise, and he acts as advisor to a number of national and international museums on their collections of African art. He is a practicing artist, who is exhibited regularly, represented in many museums, and well-known for large public commissions at home and abroad.

Mariama Ross is completing her doctorate in Art Education and African Art History at Indiana University, Bloomington. Her research interests include the interrelationships between African (Akan) cultural meanings as interpreted in visual form by contemporary Ghanaian and African American artists.

Roy Sieber, guest curator of the exhibition, is Rudy Professor Emeritus at Indiana University and has served on the faculty at numerous institutions in the United States, Nigeria and Ghana, and has engaged in field research in Nigeria and Ghana. From 1983-1993, he was Associate Director of Collections and Research at the National Museum of African Art, Smithsonian Institution. He has curated and authored accompanying catalogues of several exhibitions on African art including textiles and furniture as well as *African Art in the Cycle of Life* at the Smithsonian Institution.

William Siegmann is Curator of the Arts of Africa and the Pacific Islands at the Brooklyn Museum of Art. He lived and worked in Liberia for more than ten years where he established the Africana Museum at Cuttington University College and co-ordinated the rebuilding of the National Museum of Liberia and the development of its collections under a Fulbright grant. He has conducted field research in virtually all areas of Liberia as well as in Côte d'Ivoire, Guinea and Sierra Leone. He has also worked on museum development programs in Gabon, Sao Tomé and Guyana.

Barbara Thompson received her doctorate in African art history at the University of Iowa and will be teaching as a visiting assistant professor at the University of North Iowa. Her research concentrates on the use of arts in healing rituals in east and central Africa, with an emphasis on non-figurative, ceramic and accumulative arts.

James H. Vaughan is Professor Emeritus of Anthropology at Indiana Unitersity. He conducted four research trips among the Margi of Nigeria, beginning in 1959. His specialties have included rock art, political systems, social organizationÑincluding slavery, and demography. His most recent publication (with A. H. M. Kirk-Greene), *The Diary of Hamman Jaji: Chronicle of a West African Muslim Ruler* won the 1996 biennial prize from the African Studies Association as the best research text published in 1995.

Photo Credits

Catalogue objects by catalogue number: Dick Beaulieux 2, 6, 7, 11, 13, 14, 15, 16, 17, 18, 19, 20, 22, 23, 24, 27, 30, 32, 33, 35, 39, 40, 41, 42, 43, 44, 47, 58, 59, 64, 65, 80, 82, 84, 86, 94, 96, 98, 111d, 111e, 114, 121, 123, 126, 127, 128, 129, 131, 138, 139, 151, 154; Barbara Bourne, 76; Michael Cavanagh and Kevin Montague 21, 53, 55, 100; Don Cole, 1; Dieter Hinrichs, 54, 66, 101, 108; Franko Khoury, 38, 115, 116; Gery Mortensen, 154; Denis J. Nervig, 83, 93; Gregory Staley, 28, 36, 37, 45, 46, 51, 56, 57, 61, 62; Steven Tatum, 25; Jerry L. Thompson, 3, 4, 8, 10, 12, 24, 26, 29, 31, 34, 48, 49, 50, 52, 60, 63, 67, 68, 69, 70, 71, 72, 73, 75, 77, 78, 79, 81, 85, 87, 88, 89, 90, 91, 92, 95, 97, 99, 102, 103, 104, 105, 106, 107, 109, 110, 111a, 111b, 111c, 112, 113, 117, 118, 119, 120, 122, 124, 125, 130, 133, 134, 135, 136, 137, 140, 141, 142, 143, 144, 145, 146, 147, 148, 152, 150, 153, 155, 156, 158, 159, 160, 161, 162, 163; Ernie Wolfe Gallery, 117.

Fig. 4.   From The Secret Museum of Mankind, n.d: n.p. vol. 2, The Secret Album of Africa.
Fig. 5.   From Sabena Revue 1974: 23.
Fig. 6.   From Himmelheber 1958: no. 24c.
Fig. 7.   From Bernatzik 1929: abb. 114.
Fig. 8.   Courtesy Gamsberg Macmillan Publishers (Pty) Ltd., Windhoek, Namibia. From Scherz, et al. 1992: 69, no. 65.
Fig. 14. Casimir d'Ostoja Zagourski, 1926–1937, from the series "L'Afrique qui disparaît," no. 7, Zagourski Collection. 1987-242007, Eliot Elisofon Photographic Archives, National Museum of African Art.
Fig. 16. From Daye, et al. 1929: 10.
Fig. 17. Casimir d'Ostoja Zagourski, 1926-1937, from the series "L'Afrique qui disparaît," no. 60, Zagourski Collection. 1987-242060-01, Eliot Elisofon Photographic Archives, National Museum of African Art.
Fig. 18. From Hutchinson 1913: 735.
Fig. 19. From Himmelheber 1993: 136.
Fig. 20. From Hutchinson 1913: 822.
Fig. 22. Courtesy Gamsberg Macmillan Publishers (Pty) Ltd., Windhoek, Namibia. From Scherz, et al. 1992: 58, no.43.
Fig. 23. Courtesy of Gamsberg Macmillan Publishers (Pty) Ltd., Windhoek, Namibia. From Scherz, et al. 1992: 79, no. 86.

Fig. 25. Centro de Informação e Turismo de Angola, Gabinete Fotográfico. Courtesy Museu Nacional de Etnologia, Lisboa, Portugal.
Fig. 27. Courtesy Gamsberg Macmillan Publishers (Pty) Ltd., Windhoek, Nambia. From Scherz, et al. 1992: 53, no. 32.
Fig. 28. From Bernatzik 1933: 303, no. 379.
Fig. 29. From Bernatzik 1930: 54.
Fig. 30. From Alldridge 1901: 113, fig. 34.
Fig. 33. From Büttikofer 1890: 309.
Fig. 34. Courtesy of Brooklyn Museum of Art Library, Special Collections, Gift of James T. Garfinkel. neg. no. AAPA: Sept 1997.
Fig. 46. From Hutchinson 1913: 762.
Fig. 47. Courtesy Gamsberg Macmillan Publishers (Pty) Ltd., Windhoek, Nambia. From Scherz, et al. 1992: 81, no. 90.
Fig. 48. Courtesy Gamsberg Macmillan Publishers (Pty) Ltd., Windhoek, Nambia. From Scherz, et al. 1992: 104, no. 135.
Fig. 49. From Bernatzik 1933: 170.
Fig. 50. Courtesy Gamsberg Macmillan Publishers (Pty) Ltd., Windhoek, Nambia. From Scherz, et al. 1992: 83, no. 93.
Fig. 69. After Eve de Negri 1976:110.
Fig. 77. From Schweinfurth 1875, I: 491.
Fig. 78. From Schildkrout and Keim 1998: fig. 6.8. © Courtesy of Frobenius Institut Frankfurt, Germany.
Fig. 79. © Africa-Museum (Tervuren, Belgium), E.PH. 14422.
Fig. 80. Casimir d'Ostoja Zagourski, 1926-1937, from the series "L'Afrique qui disparaît," no. 53. Zagourski Collection, 1987-241053-01, Eliot Elisofon Photographic Archives, National Museum of African Art.
Fig. 81. Courtesy Dept. of Library Services American Museum of Natural History.
Fig. 82. © Africa-Museum (Tervuren, Belgium), E.PH. 434.
Fig. 83. Courtesy Dept. of Library Services American Museum of Natural History.
Fig. 84. © Etnographisch Museum, Antwerp, Belgium. AE 54.35.34 D.
Fig. 86. From Hutchinson 1913: 828.
Fig. 87. From Bernatzik 1933: 303, no. 378.
Fig. 89. From Hutchinson 1913: 748.

Fig. 90. Courtesy Gamsberg Macmillan Publishers (Pty) Ltd., Windhoek, Nambia. From Scherz, et al. 1992: 102, no. 133.
Fig. 91. Courtesy Gamsberg Macmillan Publishers (Pty) Ltd., Windhoek, Nambia. From Scherz, et al. 1992: 39.
Fig. 92. Courtesy Gamsberg Macmillan Publishers (Pty) Ltd., Windhoek, Nambia. From Scherz, et al. 1992: 100, no. 128.
Fig. 93. Courtesy Gamsberg Macmillan Publishers (Pty) Ltd., Windhoek, Nambia. From Scherz, et al. 1992: 61, no. 48.
Fig. 94. Centro de Informação e Turismo de Angola, Gabinete Fotográfico. Courtesy Museu Nacional de Etnologia, Lisboa, Portugal.
Fig. 95. Postcard: postmarked July 8, 1913, published by Impreimeries Reunies de Nancy, France. Postcard Collection, 1985-140027, Eliot Elisofon Photographic Archives, National Museum of African Art.
Fig. 96. From Bernatzik 1929: abb. 172.
Fig. 97. From Cudahy-Massee-Milwaukee Museum African Expedition, 1928-29: 462, fig. 387.
Fig. 98. Postcard: Published by Impreimeries Reunies de Nancy, France. Postcard Collection, 1985-140108-02, Eliot Elisofon Photographic Archives, National Museum of African Art.
Fig. 110. From Junod, 1938.
Fig. 111. From Shaw and Van Warmelo 1988.
Fig. 112. From Franck 1930: plate 74.
Fig. 113. Casimir d'Ostoja Zagourski, 1926-1937, from the series "L'Afrique qui disparaît," no. 32. Zagourski Collection, 1987-242032, Eliot Elisofon Photographic Archives, National Museum of African Art.
Fig. 114. Courtesy Gamsberg Macmillan Publishers (Pty) Ltd., Windhoek, Nambia. From Scherz, et al. 1992: 78, no. 84.
Fig. 115. Casimir d'Ostoja Zagourski, 1926-1937, from the series "L'Afrique qui disparaît," no. 139. Zagourski Collection, 1987-242139, Eliot Elisofon Photographic Archives, National Museum of African Art.

Lenders to the Exhibition

Mona Gavigan/Affrica

Kate and Ken Anderson

Corice and Armand P. Arman

Alan Brandt Inc.

Pamela and Oliver E. Cobb

Kevin Conru

Charles and Kent Davis

Woods Davy Collection

Dr. Jean and Nobel Endicott

Etnografisch Museum, Antwerp

Felix Collection

Marc and Denyse Ginzberg Collection

Graham Collection

Collection of Rita and John Grunwald

Collection of Toby and Barry Hecht

Henau Collection, Antwerp

Indiana University Art Museum

William M. Itter

Reynold C. Kerr

J.W. Mestach

Rolf and Christina Miehler

Charles D. Miller III

Mr. and Mrs. Donald Morris

Donald Morris Gallery

Amyas Naegele

National Museum of African Art

National Museum of Ethnology, Lisbon

Michael Oliver

The Saint Louis Museum of Art

Roy and Sophia Sieber

Merton Simpson Collection

Joyce Marie Sims

Thomas D. Slater

Cecilia and Irwin Smiley

Saul and Marsha Stanoff

University of Iowa Museum of Art

Ernie Wolfe Gallery, Los Angeles

Richard White

and several anonymous lenders